Hypertext and Cognition

Hypertext and Cognition

Edited by:

Jean-François Rouet
University of Poitiers

Jarmo J. Levonen
University of Pittsburgh

Andrew Dillon
Indiana University

Rand J. Spiro
University of Illinois

Routledge
Taylor & Francis Group

NEW YORK AND LONDON

First Published by
Lawrence Erlbaum Associates, Inc., Publishers
10 Industrial Avenue
Mahwah, NJ 07430

Transferred to Digital Printing 2009 by Routledge
270 Madison Ave, New York NY 10016
2 Park Square, Milton Park, Abingdon, Oxon, OX14 4RN

Cover design by Gail Silverman

Library of Congress Cataloging-in-Publication Data

Hypertext and cognition / edited by Jean-François Rouet . . . [et al.].
p.   cm.
"Originated in a symposium held in Aix-en-Provence (France) as
part of the Fifth Conference on the European Association for
Research on Learning and Instruction (EARLI)"—CIP pref.
Includes bibliographical references and index.
ISBN 0-8058-2143-0 (cloth : alk. paper). — ISBN 0-8058-2144-9
(paper : alk. paper)
1. Hypertext systems—Congresses. 2. Cognition—Congresses.
I. Rouet, Jean-François. II. European Association for Research on
Learning and Instruction. Conference (5th : 1994: Aix-en-Provence)
QA76.64.H94   1996
371.3′34575—dc20   95-41223
                                                              CIP

Publisher's Note
The publisher has gone to great lengths to ensure the quality
of this reprint but points out that some imperfections in the
original may be apparent.

Contents

Contributors

M. Anne Britt, 226 Vincent Science Hall, Slippery Rock University, Slippery Rock, PA 16057, USA

Diana Dee-Lucas, Department of Psychology, Carnegie Mellon University, Pittsburgh, PA 15213, USA

Andrew Dillon, School of Library and Information Science, Indiana University, Bloomington, IN 47405, USA

Eric Espéret, Language and Communication Laboratory, University of Poitiers and CNRS, 95 avenue du Recteur Pineau, 86022 Poitiers Cedex, France

Peter W. Foltz, Department of Psychology, New Mexico State University, Box 30001, Dept. 3452, Las Cruces, NM 88003, USA

Jarmo J. Levonen, Learning Research and Development Center, University of Pittsburgh, 3939 O'Hara Street, Pittsburgh, PA 15260, USA

Charles A. Perfetti, Learning Research and Development Center, University of Pittsburgh, 3939 O'Hara Street, Pittsburgh, PA 15260, USA

Jean-François Rouet, Language and Communication Laboratory, University of Poitiers and CNRS, 95 avenue du Recteur Pineau, 86022 Poitiers Cedex, France

Rand J. Spiro, Center for the Study of Reading, University of Illinois, Urbana-Champaign, 210b Education Building, MC 708, 1310 S. Sixth, Champaign, IL 61820, USA

Herre van Oostendorp, Department of Psychonomics, Utrecht University, Heidelberglaan 2, 3584 CS Utrecht, The Netherlands

Preface

The idea of this volume originated in a symposium held in Aix-en-Provence (France) as part of the Fifth Conference of the European Association for Research on Learning and Instruction (EARLI). This meeting provided us with an opportunity to share our interests in hypertext and its applications in education and information usage. It also made it clear to us that a volume presenting quality empirical evidence and theoretical contributions on this topic was missing. The quality of the presentations presented at the symposium, and also the spirited mood that resulted from the discussions (see Perfetti's La Maison Hypertext), encouraged us to engage in the venture. Following the meeting, an Editorial Board was put together and several researchers were invited to submit chapters presenting theoretical and/or empirical contributions on the topic of Hypertext and Cognition. The present volume is the result of a careful process of submission, reviewing, and editing of the chapters. We hope that it will contribute to a better understanding of the potential of hypertext technologies. The editors and the authors of *Hypertext and Cognition* are grateful to Lawrence Erlbaum Associates for their support and patience during the complex and nonlinear process of putting together this volume.

Jean-François Rouet
Jarmo J. Levonen
Andrew Dillon
Rand J. Spiro

La Maison Hypertext

Charles A. Perfetti
University of Pittsburgh

CARTE

Les Potages

Bisque de Constructionisme	25 francs
Potage Hypertext à la Provençale	19

Hors D'Oeuvres

Salade de Vérités Eternelles	24
Concombres à la Crême Nonlinear	15
Filets d'Anchois au Beurre Associationist	17

Les Poissons

Sole Rouet	69
Turbot Grillé Sauce Flexibilité	74
Huitres à la MacIntosh	50

1

▼▼▼▼▼▼▼

An Introduction to Hypertext and Cognition

Jean-François Rouet
University of Poitiers and CNRS, Poitiers Cedex France

Jarmo J. Levonen
University of Pittsburgh

Andrew Dillon
Indiana University

Rand J. Spiro
University of Illinois, Urbana-Champaign

The recent evolution of Western societies has been characterized by an increasing emphasis on the importance of information and communication. This is equally true at the workplace, at school, and at home where the amount of information available through books, journals, TV, and other media is growing exponentially. It is likely that this evolution will lead to some form of crisis, which may even have already started. As the amount of available information increases, the user—worker, student, or citizen—will face new problems in selecting and accessing relevant information. It is more than ever crucial to find efficient ways that allow users to interact with information systems in a way that prevents them from being overwhelmed or from just missing their targets.

Hypertext systems have been proposed as a means of facilitating the interactions between readers and texts. In hypertext, information is organized as a network in which nodes are text chunks (e.g., lists of items, paragraphs, pages) and links are relationships between the nodes (e.g., semantic associations, expansions, definitions, examples; virtually any kind of relation that can be imagined between two text passages). This simple idea has long historical roots, usually traced to Vannevar Bush (1945), but really beginning much farther back in history with the first writers and manuscript designers. Bush dreamed of the technology to handle the material, and the computer provided the most appropriate means of realizing these dreams, but the idea that the basis of organization influences the use of information is an old one indeed.

As with any interactive computer applications, a hypertext system includes an interface which allows the user to select a node, read it, and move from there to one of the linked nodes. There are many ways in which a hypertext interface can be designed, and so far, a large part of the hypertext research effort has consisted of proposing all sorts of techniques, tricks, and oddities under the label "hypertext tools." As a result, the complexity of some hypertext interfaces extends far beyond the processing capacities of regular users, which brings us back to the starting point; users being overwhelmed by the amount of information to process. It is becoming widely recognized that a more rational approach based on a thorough analysis of an information user's needs, capacities, capabilities, and skills is needed. The present volume seeks to meet that need.

SYSTEM VERSUS USER-CENTERED PERSPECTIVES ON HYPERTEXT

From the start, hypertext research has brought together researchers from different fields. The first international conference on hypertext held in Chapel Hill in 1987 involved people from computer science, education, psychology, linguistics, and graphic design among others, although in unequal numbers. This "native" interdisciplinarity has continued to characterize the following meetings, although most conferences have been dominated by the computer science community.

Generally speaking, there are two main perspectives on hypertext research; a system-centered perspective and a user-centered perspective.

The system-centered perspective pays attention to the invention and implementation of hypertext techniques. Concern is expressed about the machine processing routines, possible architectures, and document transfer. Important issues from this perspective are how to store and manipulate data sets, linking mechanisms, retrieval algorithms, and so on. Less attention is paid to the actual use of the proposed systems or techniques than to the technological requirements of handling hypertextual data. For instance, researchers rarely conduct field or even laboratory studies to check the usability of their work, and tend to concentrate more on demonstrating a system's potential. This perspective has been largely dominant in hypertext research.

The user-centered perspective focuses on the interactions between a system and its users. It is concerned with the skills required to use the system and the effects of the system on people's activities. From this perspective, less attention is paid to the technical characteristics of the system unless the researcher wants to check the effects of one specific feature on the user, and more attention is spent on identifying the problems users are likely to experience.

Of course the distinction between system- and user-centered hypertext research is not totally clear-cut, and many researchers are actually interested in both. Still, the two perspectives use quite different theoretical backgrounds and methods. For instance, papers written in the first perspective rarely make reference to psychological theories, or contain any data from studies involving end users. Conversely, papers in the second perspective rarely contain any new hypertext technique or tackle software engineering problems, but merely make use of existing systems to investigate user responses to hypertext structures.

PRESENTATION OF THE VOLUME

This volume clearly follows the second research perspective. Its purpose is to present theoretical and empirical research studies on the cognitive processes involved in using hypertext. We consider a sound psychological theory of hypertext usage a prerequisite to rational hypertext design.

Yet, even labeling a perspective user centered hides many divisions among its adherents. Within the present volume alone, which we see as mirroring the field at large, we can identify three main approaches.

First is the approach of cognitive science. There have been many studies of how people read and learn from conventional, printed text (e.g., Mandl, Stein, & Trabasso, 1984; van Dijk & Kintsch, 1983). These studies provide basic models for hypertext processing by grounding our understanding and analysis of reading in the methods and constructs of psychological research. Especially important is the notion that text comprehension is a multilayered cognitive activity that occurs in the context of a limited-capacity working memory. A consequence is that readers have to manage their cognitive resources in order to process a text continuously and achieve the best learning outcomes. These notions also apply in the case of hypertext. However, hypertext also involves specific reading strategies, due to its computer-based and nonlinear format (see Dillon's chapter and Espéret's discussion for a counterargument on linearity). Thus, a comprehensive model of reading hypertext should integrate basic text comprehension mechanisms with the specific strategies required by this presentation.

A second approach is provided by the field of ergonomics or human factors (e.g., Dillon, 1994). Reading a hypertext can be seen as a situated interaction between a user and a complex device. Several characteristics of the user and the device influence the interaction between them. On the user side, parameters such as training, cognitive abilities, and expertise in the domain influence the way people use textual information. On the system side, many design options (e.g., quality of the display, number, shape and location of text windows, navigation tools, information structure) included in the hypertext can influence the reader's activity. Again, empirical studies are necessary to get a precise picture of these mutual influences for any given context of usage.

The third approach is provided by the field of education where hypertext has a major appeal for the provision and support of learning environments offering new possibilities for pedagogy (e.g., Jonassen, 1989). Educationalists focus on issues such as understanding organizational parameters (single or cooperative use), the type of learning objectives, the frequency and duration of the hypertext sessions, the type of reading activity, and the learning characteristics and needs of the users (e.g., normal vs. poor readers or learners).

What links all these perspectives in the present volume is the fact that the authors see hypertext as more than just a presentation medium: It is also a useful vehicle for testing the theoretical models derived from their respective fields or approaches. Thus, as a sort of experimental paradigm based on psychological theory, hypertext enables us to rapidly implement text structures which can be evaluated for their cognitive, ergonomic, and educational implications. As such, hypertext extends the tradition of experimental work on reading, offering an exciting and infinite range of possibilities for empirical work which tests our current understanding of the reading process to the limits. If nothing else, hypertext provides a common testing ground for the cognitivists and the constructivists, educationalists and information scientists, computer scientists and human scientists.

Specific Themes

This volume addresses several important issues for hypertext research.

The first issue may be labeled "What is hypertext good for?" The analysis of tasks and activities for which hypertext may be relevant and useful has to date been surprisingly shallow. A popular claim is that hypertext can be very useful for learning and instruction. But what type of learning and instruction are we talking about? And how can hypertext be used in this context? Several chapters in the present volume attempt to provide more consistent analyses of this issue. Rouet and Levonen review empirical research on hypertext usage and identify several factors that may influence the efficiency of hypertext. Dillon challenges several myths related to hypertext usage and proposes a general framework within which to characterize the interactions between readers and documents from a cognitive ergonomics and task-centered point of view. Foltz points out the readers' need for textual coherence both in printed text and hypertext. Dee-Lucas demonstrates that the effectiveness of hypertext presentation varies as a function of task demands, and interprets her findings within the current cognitive models of text comprehension. Finally, van Oostendorp explores the issues of integrating notetaking facilities in an electronic information system. His results do not indicate any positive or negative influence of such a facility on students' learning from electronic text. The use of an electronic pencil by inexperienced subjects led to as accurate a text editing as editing with paper and pencil.

The second issue may be labeled "Who is hypertext good for?" Assuming the proper situational context (i.e., a satisfactory answer to the issue raised in the previous paragraph), would any regular reader benefit from using a hypertext system? Anyone who has ever observed students interacting with a computer application may guess that the answer is negative, for several reasons.

One reason is that there are huge individual differences in the way people interact with information systems. Confronted with an information search task, for instance, it is rare that two readers or searchers will display the exact same pattern of selections. The studies reported here by Britt, Rouet, and Perfetti illustrate the variability of college students' strategies in a simple hypertext environment. Students' selections are opportunistic and relatively unaffected by discipline expertise.

Another reason is that practice in the use of a device generally results in an important evolution in the users' behavior. When we search for usable solutions in design, we must be careful not to equate usability with learnability as so often seems to occur. Dillon's chapter outlines several variables, such as the information model developed by the reader, or their interpretation of the task and its resolution, that must change over time.

An overarching question is "What particular cognitive skills are needed in order to interact successfully with a hypertext system?" To answer this question, it is necessary to build up a detailed theoretical representation of the psychological processes that underlie this type of interaction. Again, several of the chapters presented in this volume address this question and provide elements for an answer. In their review of the literature, Rouet and Levonen discuss the problem of the user's navigation in hypertext. Dillon raises the issue of a reader's perceiving structure in discourse. Foltz points out the need for coherence both in printed text and hypertext, and shows how readers tend to stick to subjectively coherent patterns when they navigate hypertext hierarchies. Finally, Britt, Rouet, and Perfetti show the students' need for coherence and their preference for top-level representations (e.g., a structured table of contents) over embedded links. Each of these issues suggests part of the required answer.

Perspectives

Although we have tried to provide a comprehensive view on the issue of hypertext and cognition, we do not pretend that all the relevant issues are covered (see the critical discussions by Eric Espéret and Charles Perfetti). In particular, very little is known regarding the consequences of hypertext usage in terms of information processing skills. Can hypertext transform the way people interact with information sources? Can it be used to develop efficient strategies in students? The studies presented here leave these two questions unanswered.

Another unanswered question concerns the limits of hypertext usage. Are there any application domains or types of activity where hypertext should never be employed? Is it incompatible with the organization of some information structures or some tasks? Pushed for an answer, our liberal dispositions suggest that there can be no such limits placed on hypertext because the potential for better design is infinite, but we cannot yet justify this answer through recourse to the scientific base, where evidence to date has raised some serious doubts about the claims made for this medium.

Most of the research studies presented in this volume benefited from hypertext as a research device and model. Experimental hypertext systems were used to collect protocols of subjects' information processing strategies (through their selections and time allocation). These records are a valuable source of information for research on higher level processes involved in information usage. In this way, the ultimate message of this volume may be that there can be a cross-fertilization of technological advances on the one hand, and research on the nature of the human mind on the other hand. If our technologies are truly embodiments of our theories as Dillon notes, then the explosion in information technology that we are witnessing suggests interesting times ahead for researchers, developers, and users. But we must seek to shape this future actively, not just let it occur. The message of this volume is that the experimental, user-based approach offers the best method that we possess for technology shaping.

REFERENCES

Bush, V. (1945). As we may think. *Atlantic Monthly, 176*(1), 101–108.
Dillon, A. (1994). *Designing usable electronic text: Ergonomic aspects of human information usage.* Bristol, PA: Taylor and Francis.
Jonassen, D. (1989). *Hypertext/Hypermedia.* Englewood Cliffs, NJ: Educational Technology Publications.
Mandl, H., Stein, N., & Trabasso, T. (Eds.). (1985). *Learning and comprehension of text.* Hillsdale, NJ: Lawrence Erlbaum Associates.
van Dijk, T. A., & Kintsch, W. (1983). *Strategies of discourse comprehension.* Hillsdale, NJ: Lawrence Erlbaum Associates.

2
▼▼▼▼▼▼

Studying and Learning With Hypertext: Empirical Studies and Their Implications

Jean-François Rouet
CNRS and University of Poitiers

Jarmo J. Levonen
University of Pittsburgh

Recent years have seen a blossoming of computerized systems that allow new ways of presenting information; hypertext, hypermedia, and multimedia systems. A common attribute of these systems is nonlinearity, or the networking of information units. Instead of looking at a predefined sequence of text, pictures, or graphics, the reader or learner is enabled to build his or her own paths, to select and organize the information relevant to his or her needs or objectives. Let us examine more closely what is meant by "linear" versus "nonlinear" organization of information.

In traditional media, information is organized linearly; that is, information units are arranged in predefined sequences. This is true of sentences in a paragraph, paragraphs in a chapter, chapters in a book. Linearity is also a characteristic of newer media such as television or radio. For instance, when presented with a news broadcast, the viewer or listener has no way to select a priori a subset of information or to rearrange the order of presentation. For this reason, linearity is often seen as a constraint inherent to traditional media that limits people's ability to interact with information.

However, linear does not mean arbitrary. Information producers use a tremendous amount of expertise (knowledge, skill, imagination) when creating information sequences. They use data about who will use the information, how, and for what purpose. They also use some knowledge about basic information processing mechanisms, although most often they do so implicitly. For instance, text authors usually try to maximize text coherence, news broadcasters try not to overload the viewer, and so forth. It should be noted that from a cognitive standpoint, the nature of the expertise involved in creating optimal sequences of information for a specific audience or situation is still largely unknown. But in any case, everyday experience demonstrates that communicating through text, speech, images, and so on involves lots of knowledge and skill.

Despite all this know-how, it is sometimes hard to reconcile the multidimensional organization of concepts in a knowledge domain with the constraints of traditional media. For instance, open a newspaper dealing with a major political event, say the Bosnia–Herzegovina crisis. You may find a summary of recent events in Sarajevo, an interview of a Serbian leader, a report on life conditions in a besieged Muslim area, an update on peace talks, and so on. All these pieces of information contribute to an understanding of the situation, and they can be related in multiple ways. But there is no absolute optimal ordering of them, nor is there any optimal level of detail at which to present them. It all depends on who reads, how, and for what purpose. The best thing a newspaper page can do is to provide an approximation of nonlinearity, given the constraints of a two-dimensional medium: The result is often a two-dimensional mess.

For more than 50 years, since Bush wrote his now classic paper on "As we may think" (Bush, 1945), there has been an intuition that computer systems, with their capacity of quickly selecting, retrieving, and arranging data, may facilitate the interactions of information and information users. Hypertext[1] as we know it today can be seen as an attempt to implement that intuition.

Hypertexts have become increasingly popular in the areas of information science and educational research. Journals, conferences, and workshops have been set up to allow the diffusion of hypertext research. Many experimental hypertext systems have been developed and some are available as commercial products. Hypertext-based applications are now available for industry and education. But what about the impact of hypertext on information processing and learning? To what extent does hypertext succeed in easing the reader's access to and processing of information?

So far, the focus of hypertext research has been on the development of new systems in a rather nontheoretical, technology-driven way. There have been few attempts to study the cognitive processes involved in reading hypertext or to provide controlled evaluations of the impact of hypertext on learning. Therefore, little is known about the effectiveness of hypertext as a learning tool. Chances are that the lack of theoretical foundations and empirical evidence will eventually hinder further developments in the design of hypertext technologies.

It may be argued that hypertext is such a versatile concept that it cannot be evaluated per se. Granted, a hypertext system can be used in a variety of ways (e.g.,

---

[1]In this chapter, we use the word hypertext as a generic name for nonlinear information systems, whether or not they may include nontextual information. However, as with most chapters in this volume, we focus primarily on text-only applications.

as a card system, as a help system, as a library system, or as a database search system). However, it is likely that the use of hypertext involves a set of basic cognitive processes and strategies, regardless of the context. Empirical studies are essential to identify these processes and to find out how they are affected by particular design features. Such data can provide input for general cognitive models of linear and nonlinear information processing. Empirical studies may also help explain when and how nonlinear documents can fruitfully support learning activities (Rouet, 1992). Finally, empirical studies may allow hypertext developers to make design decisions based on the needs of users rather than on fuzzy principles or mere intuition (Dillon, Richardson, & McKnight, 1989).

The most obvious outcome one can expect from empirical studies is an assessment of hypertext effectiveness compared to other media. However, the issue of hypertext usability cannot be reduced to simple comparisons between "linear" and "nonlinear" presentations of the same materials. Evaluating hypertext requires a multifactorial approach, taking into account user characteristics, the type of task performed, and design options (Rouet, 1992; Wright, 1991). As a matter of fact, empirical studies conducted so far have addressed a variety of hypertext-related issues with the aid of diverse methods. They have involved different populations, ranging from young, inexperienced hypertext readers (e.g., Rouet, 1990) to more expert populations (McKnight, Dillon, & Richardson, 1990).

Studies have also examined the use of different systems with variable design options. Some studies have examined full-size hypertext applications (e.g., Rada & Murphy, 1992). Others have used smaller hypertexts designed specially for the purpose of experimentation (e.g., Dee-Lucas & Larkin, 1992).

Finally, several studies have focused on the reading task of the user, such as general comprehension (Gordon, Gustavel, Moore, & Hankey, 1988), question answering or fact retrieval (Gray & Shasha, 1989), along with different dependent measures (online data, recall, or comprehension measures).

Rationale of the Chapter

In this chapter, we focus on a few central issues that have emerged from the studies conducted so far and illustrate how empirical work contributes to resolve them. Our main concern is the use of hypertext by actual readers or learners, especially those with little initial expertise of hypertext.

In the next section, we review some theoretical conceptions of hypertext. The following two sections examine some of the issues that have been studied empirically. We summarize their main outcomes with an emphasis on the instructional use of hypertext. In the fourth section, we consider different ways to improve hypertext effectiveness. We try to analyze the type of skills that are needed for an efficient use of hypertext, and how these skills are learned by inexperienced hypertext readers.

IS HYPERTEXT A HYPER-TEXT? ANALOGIES, METAPHORS, AND BEYOND

A major drawback of current hypertext research is its lack of a thorough theoretical foundation. There is neither a general theory of hypertext, nor a model of the cognitive processes involved in reading hypertext. There is a large gap between theories of knowledge or discourse and the actual hypertext systems. The gap is even larger between those systems and models of reading and comprehension processes. Given this lack of foundation, researchers have tried to characterize hypertext by pointing out its similarities and differences with linear (printed) text. Analogies and metaphors play a central role in these efforts to understand the specificity of hypertext.

Like many other computer applications, hypertext shares many features with the traditional technology it is supposed to enhance, that is, printed text. The user of a hypertext reads information printed on "pages," and progresses by going from one page to the other. Many hypertexts also include the electronic equivalent to a table of contents or an index. However, the analogy between traditional text and hypertext is limited by two specific features of hypertext: Pages in hypertext are organized in a network, as opposed to a sequence in printed books; and the progression in hypertext is user controlled, as opposed to predefined by the author.

These features not only affect the reading process, but also how a reader represents the hypertext structure. Whereas the semantic macro-organization of a book—sections and subsections—is explicit and obviously identical across readers, "organization" in a hypertext depends on each user's progression and understanding.

There is controversy over the amount of "freedom" that comes with using hypertext. A popular view is that reading is less constrained in hypertext than in printed text, because hypertext allows several ways to linearize information. Thus, hypertext readers are free to organize a personalized path through the information network. However, some authors (e.g., Duchastel, 1986) have pointed out that computerized text limits the range of possible reading strategies. With printed text, a reader can go literally from anywhere to anywhere; in hypertext, progression is bound by the definition of textual units (pages isolated from each other) and by the existence of links between units. Links are often the only way to navigate a hypertext, thus limiting the possibilities to jump from page to page.

In fact, the difference is not so much in the potential freedom that text or hypertext allows but rather in the way readers actually use this freedom. With printed text, the reader can passively follow the organization proposed by the author. On the contrary, progression in hypertext requires active decision making on the part of the reader. After each and every unit of information, the reader must select a target node in order to progress. In order to make coherent selections, the reader has to possess a mental representation of how the information is organized. Because hypertext is a new medium, such a representation must rely on concepts that readers are already familiar with, hence the use of metaphors. It is well known that metaphors help make computer applications understandable and acceptable to novice users. Designers of new computer applications have to refer to existing or known objects, even though this may limit the power of the application (Brown, 1992).

Hypertext is often referred to as a "space" in which the readers "navigate" according to their objectives. Dillon, McKnight, and Richardson (1990) studied the relationships between navigation in physical space and hypertext. Navigation in physical spaces involves four levels of representation; schemata, landmarks, routes, and surveys. Learning to navigate a hypertext may involve similar levels. However, Dillon, McKnight, and Richardson (1993) have also pointed out that although the notion of navigation is a useful metaphor, the conception of hypertext as a "semantic space" is not realistic. Semantic space is "an abstract psycholinguistic concept which cannot be directly observed" (p. 186). People do not navigate semantic space, but its physical representations (printed or electronic texts) which are constrained and rather impoverished.

Beyond images such as the space metaphor, there have been few attempts to provide broader theoretical views on reading hypertext. A notable exception is the work of Spiro and colleagues (Spiro, 1993; Spiro, Coulson, Feltovich, & Anderson, 1988; Spiro, Feltovitch, Jacobson, & Coulson, 1991). They proposed the Cognitive Flexibility Theory (CFT), a set of principles to account for advanced learning in ill-structured domains (e.g., biomedicine or social sciences). Based on their observations of students' failure to acquire advanced knowledge, Spiro et al. (1991) claimed that "revisiting the same material, at different times, in re-arranged contexts, for different purposes, and from different conceptual perspectives is essential for attaining the goals of advanced knowledge acquisition" (p. 28).

According to Spiro et al., hypertext is a suitable medium to support these activities because it allows a multiple structuring of contents. Indeed, in a study by Jacobson and Spiro (1991), a hypertext designed according to the cognitive flexibility principles enhanced the transfer of learning across situations, whereas a computer-based drill covering the same contents promoted memory for facts.

In a few other cases, the design of hypertext systems has been inspired by theoretical models of discourse processing. The SEPIA system (Streitz, Hanneman, & Thüring, 1989) supports the development of hypertexts based on the Toulmin (1958) model of argumentation (see also Schuler & Smith, 1990).

In the two following sections, we study in more detail how nonlinear presentation of information can influence the processes of reading and comprehending text. To begin with, we study the influence of "nonlinear adjuncts" (e.g., definitions) on the comprehension of computerized linear text. Then, we examine the problem of reading text networks, with an emphasis on the "disorientation problem."

MAKING LINEAR TEXT "HYPER": ONLINE AIDS
TO TEXT COMPREHENSION

There is no absolute boundary between linear text and hypertext. In fact, even printed text often includes nonlinear features. Technical or expository text, for instance, is not always meant to be read from beginning to end. Lengthy texts include structural information such as a table of contents or an index that allows the reader to locate directly the passages of interest. Textbooks and manuals also frequently include various types of embedded documents (e.g., pictures, graphics, or tables). When encountering a reference to an embedded document, the reader must decide whether to examine the embedded document or to continue reading the text. Footnotes, glossaries, and dictionaries are other widespread examples of adjunct information that makes printed text nonlinear.

All these nonlinear features aim at facilitating the understanding of a text. However, the availability of such information is no guarantee that it will be used effectively by readers. Readers, especially younger students, may not be aware of the benefits of reading a document or checking word definitions. Furthermore, jumping to a document or picking up a dictionary can disrupt the process of comprehending the main text.

There have been several attempts to find out whether computerized presentation can promote the use of nonlinear features included in otherwise linear text. Online presentations of definitions, for example, may be less disruptive than paper presentations because the computer can perform the definition search for the reader. Reinking and Rickman (1990) asked 5th and 6th graders to study a short science text in one of four presentation conditions; printed text with a dictionary, printed text with a glossary of selected terms, computerized text with either optional or mandatory definitions. Subjects in the computer-optional definitions conditions were much more willing to read word definitions than subjects in the printed glossary condition. Furthermore, the two computer conditions resulted in better vocabulary learning than did their paper counterparts.

The way definitions are presented on the computer display also plays an important role in readers' willingness to examine them. Black, Wright, Black, and Norman (1992) demonstrated that highlighting the defined items and having definitions directly accessible on the main screen (as opposed to on a separate index) increased the frequency of definition use. Black et al. suggested that the "cognitive cost," or mental effort required to access definitions might be a key factor. For instance, when definitions are presented on a separate glossary, readers have trouble relocating themselves in the main text (see also Wright, 1991).

The notion of making linear text easier to understand by including on-demand definitions raises a further problem; the writer must decide which terms are worth defining (i.e., which ones will be highlighted, clickable, etc.). Lachman (1989) asked 32 college students to read a textbook chapter presented page by page on a computer screen. Each page included one word or phrase whose definition could be called for. Based on van Dijk and Kintsch's (1983) model of discourse comprehension, the defined words were either textually important or less important. Students reading the chapter with important definitions tended to select more definitions. They also obtained better scores on a comprehension posttest. Lachman's study illustrates the importance of using psycholinguistic models when designing computerized information systems (Espéret, 1992).

Another way to make text processing nonlinear is to allow the reader to take notes while reading. Van Oostendorp (in this volume) reported evidence that note taking while reading promotes text comprehension. He designed a series of experiments to determine whether the benefits of note taking are enhanced by a computerized reading/notetaking facility. However, compared to a paper and pencil situation, computer note taking while reading did not result in any difference in text comprehension. In contrast to online definition studies (Black et al., 1992), interface manipulations did not result in any performance differences either.

Although the advantage of computer presentation was not evidenced in this case, van Oostendorp suggested that the results are nevertheless promising, given subjects' lack of computer experience. A study by Smeaton (1991) supported similar conclusions. Fifty college students used a hypertext as part of a computer science course on databases. The students were then asked to evaluate the system. One of the most frequent requests and suggestions for improvements was the possibility to annotate or take notes while studying. Note taking seems to be an important component of text-based learning, especially when the material to be learned is lengthy and complex (in the Smeaton study, the hypertext included 462 nodes and 1398 links).

Two main conclusions can be drawn from these studies. First, there may not be such a fundamental difference between printed and electronic text as far as linearity is concerned. Nonlinearity can be introduced in varying degrees and levels in both computer and paper presentations. However, a major benefit of computer presentation is that it can make it easier for readers to take advantage of the nonlinear features included.

Second, it seems that readers can benefit from moderate degrees of nonlinearity, for example, online definitions. Accessing extra information while reading can compensate for initial deficiencies in vocabulary or background knowledge. However, comprehension is a continuous process, and interruptions can be harmful (Dee-Lucas & Larkin, 1992). Computerized presentation can decrease the cost of accessing extra information and thus facilitate comprehension of unfamiliar text (Wright, 1991).

NAVIGATING TEXT NETWORKS:
IS THERE A DISORIENTATION PROBLEM?

The data presented in the previous section have illustrated that there is no absolute distinction between linear and nonlinear text. However, the prototypical representation of hypertext is a set of text units connected through multiple links, that is, a text network. Text networks are supposed to allow readers to select, read, and review only the subset of information that matches their needs or objectives. However, there is no consensus on how easy, enjoyable, and efficient it is to read and learn from text networks.

It is not the case that this problem has been ignored or overlooked in the literature. In fact, authors have been prolific at expressing theses, views, or opinions on the issue. But, ideology has often been substituted for scientific investigation, and although the hypertext literature is crowded with strong claims, rigorous empirical demonstrations are harder to find.

Advocates of hypertext have argued that hypertext navigation is not a serious problem. Landow (1991) considered that "navigation and orientation are simply pseudo-problems" (p. 364). Brown (as cited in Dillon et al., 1993) claimed that "in some smallish applications [getting lost] is not a major problem at all" (p. 171). Bernstein, Joyce, and Levine (1992) suggested that recurrence, for example, the action of revisiting hypertext nodes cannot be taken as evidence for disorientation: "In small hypertexts, to be sure, recurrence is boring. Recurrence is unhelpful, too, in encyclopedias and reference manuals which are meant to be consulted in brief episodes. In complex hypertexts, on the other hand, recurrence is not a defect; repetition provides a powerful structural force, a motif which helps readers synthesize the experience of the reading. Rhythms of recurrence announce patterns of meaning" (p. 163).

These views are interesting from an aesthetic or literary point of view. However, from a cognitive standpoint, they do not provide any evidence of how actual readers experience navigation in hypertext. In fact, a closer look at the literature shows that hypertext readers, especially novice ones, may indeed experience disorientation and navigation problems.

In a study by Foss (1989, experiment 1), hypertext readers tended to "loop" in the hypertext, and to flip through pages instead of reading them carefully. Self-reports indicated that looping and flipping did not reflect deliberate strategies but resulted from a disorientation problem. Subjects reported difficulties in defining an optimal reading order, and in locating themselves in the network (see also Edwards & Hardman, 1989).

Gray (1990) reported a study in which 10 subjects read a 68-unit hypertext with the goal of answering questions. Think aloud protocols were recorded during hypertext navigation and matched to the subjects' selections in the hypertext. The subjects experienced several types of navigation problems: Some subjects could not remember what they had and had not read, they lacked organizational cues, and they were not sure where to find the information they needed. When asked to draw a representation of the hypertext structure, subjects tended to reproduce conventional patterns such as sequences, simple hierarchies, and tables. Gray concluded that novice hypertext users need analogies with conventional structures, but, that with some training, hypertext users might become able to deal with loosely structured materials.

McKnight, Dillon, and Richardson (1990) provided evidence of disorientation problems in a hypertext search task. They asked a group of 16 adults to answer a series of 12 questions by searching a 40-card document. The document was presented in one of four formats; two hypertexts and two linear formats (paper and word processor). Search time was similar in the four conditions, but linear documents resulted in better answers. In the hypertext conditions, the subjects spent a greater proportion of time searching the menus, and rarely used the direct links between cards. The authors concluded that inexperienced hypertext users face a task management problem: The powerful search facilities offered by hypertext are not spontaneously used in optimal ways.

Disorientation can be observed even in very simple hypertexts. Rouet (1990) asked middle school students to read a hypertext made of six text passages and a single menu. Students were instructed to browse the hypertext until they had visited each unit at least once. Students' navigation patterns varied in the number and order of text selections. Some students read each unit just once, in an order that reflected semantic relations between topics. Other students went back several times to the same units ("looping"), and did not follow the relations between units ("jumping"). The findings indicated that looping and jumping did not result from deliberate strategies, but reflected students' disorientation. Looping decreased when navigation was made easier by marking previous selections or by making the relations between units explicit. Furthermore, in a second session, the students' selections followed more closely the relations between units, indicating that familiarity influenced their navigation strategies.

These studies show that navigating a text network is a complex cognitive activity. Compared to linear text, hypertext imposes a higher cognitive load on the reader: The reader must remember her location in the network, make decisions about where to go next, and keep track of pages previously visited (Wright, 1991). Under these conditions, it is hardly surprising that empirical comparisons between paper presentation (a familiar situation) and hypertext (a new, cognitively demanding situation) do not always favor hypertext. However, this does not mean that hypertext cannot be useful in certain situations. But empirical studies point out the necessity of being aware of the needs of readers when designing complex information systems. In the next section, we illustrate how research findings may improve hypertext effectiveness.

STRUCTURE, COHERENCE, AND EXPERTISE; THREE STEPS TOWARD EFFICIENT HYPERTEXTS

The research studies reviewed in the previous sections indicate three ways to improve hypertext design. One way is to provide structural cues to the reader, a second way is to improve the coherence of information in hypertext, and a third way is to provide the reader with adequate reading skills and strategies through familiarization and training procedures.

Provide Structure

Text comprehension research has demonstrated the importance of providing the reader with structural cues. Headings, connectives, and other text organizers facilitate text comprehension (Mayer, 1984; Spyridakis & Standal, 1987). As evidenced in many studies, a basic problem with hypertext is the lack of organizational cues. It is important for the reader to know her current location in the network, to keep track of previous steps, and to locate target nodes easily. With respect to these requirements, structural cues may be an important factor of hypertext readability.

Indeed, some studies have shown that structuring hypertext improves subjects' performance. For instance, structured representations of the hypertext contents facilitates subjects' orientation. Dee-Lucas and Larkin (1992, experiment 1) asked college students to study a nine-unit document dealing with basic electricity concepts. The text was presented on a computer screen in either a linear or a hypertext format. Furthermore, two versions of the hypertext were prepared. In the unstructured version, hypertext units were accessible through an alphabetic index. In the structured version, the index was organized hierarchically. Both hypertext conditions resulted in a larger breadth of recall, that is, subjects were able to recall information from more text units. Furthermore, selections were faster in the hierarchical than in the alphabetic index. Subjects also recalled better the organization of titles in the hierarchical index (see also Happ & Stanners, 1991).

These results are consistent with those reported by Simpson and McKnight (1990), who observed facilitation effects of a hierarchical index compared to an alphabetic index: Subjects using the hierarchical index had more efficient navigation patterns. They also gave better answers to content questions and were better at reconstructing the hypertext structure. Another study by Mohageg (1992) showed that a hierarchical linking structure allowed a faster search than either a linear or network organization. Hierarchical representations may help readers build up mental maps of hypertext structure (Dillon, McKnight, & Richardson, 1990).

All these studies show that structural cues facilitate navigation in hypertext. However, the effect of different presentation formats depends on the reading task. Dee-Lucas and Larkin (1992, experiment 2) found that a more specific reading task (reading to summarize the document) decreased the differences between presentation formats. The authors concluded that the subjects' greater involvement in the learning task could overcome the influence of different presentation formats (see also Lehtinen, Balcytiene, & Gustafsson, 1993). Moreover, it is important to ensure the compatibility of different structural cues. For instance, Tripp and Robby (1990) found that two types of cues (graphical metaphor and advance organizers) had positive effects when presented in isolation, but not when used in combination. The authors suggested that different types of cues may trigger different representation modes that may not be compatible with each other.

Provide Coherence

Text coherence plays a central role in building up a mental representation of the text content. In hypertext, the semantic relations between units are not always explicitly represented. Therefore, hypertext readers may make incoherent transitions between hypertext units. Foltz (1992, experiment 2) asked 6 undergraduates to study an introductory economics chapter using a hierarchical hypertext system, with either a specific goal ($n = 2$) or a general goal ($n = 4$). Think-aloud protocols recorded during the reading task indicated that subjects used strategies to maintain coherence in the information they processed. For instance, after making cross-hierarchical moves, subjects tended to go back to the previous section read in order to reinstate a context. Subjects also relied heavily on the hypertext map for orientation. These data confirm that readers have a strong need for coherence when studying complex materials (see also Foltz, this volume).

In some cases, hypertext can be used to support the study of multiple documents related to a problem. Rouet, Britt, Mason, and Perfetti (1992) used a simple hypertext system to present college students with a set of texts and documents related to a historical controversy. Each document was accessible independently and was presented linearly. In this case, the internal coherence of each text passage was maintained, and the hypertext system was used to present several documents in an integrated way. In the Rouet et al. study, subjects did not report any problem in using the system and managed to keep good track of the information sources after the study period. However, there was no attempt to compare directly the efficiency of hypertext and paper presentation (see Britt, Rouet, & Perfetti, this volume).

Provide Expertise

In the research conducted to date, one important factor may have been overlooked: Subjects have had no prior knowledge or practice of reading nonlinear materials. Here again, research on printed text provides ample evidence that text comprehension and text learning require sophisticated cognitive strategies on the part of the reader (Garner, 1987). Individuals devote a great deal of time and effort to acquire efficient reading skills. However, for the average reader, these skills are closely dependent on familiar text structures. Think, for instance, of the hardships that even mature readers face when trying to make sense out of unfamiliar text structures such as technical or legal documents. Not only is the domain unfamiliar, but these documents use special writing styles and even special presentation formats that are a challenge even for experienced readers.

Reading and using hypertext is similar to using a very unfamiliar type of text. The readers have to acquire specific strategies, such as knowing where they are, deciding where to go next, and building a cognitive representation of the network structure, in order to cope with the specific constraints of nonlinear presentation.

Studies by Rouet (1990, 1991) have shown that young students' strategies in navigating hypertexts are quite low at first. But these strategies improve dramatically within a few training sessions. Students learn to consider relationships between units (Rouet, 1990), and to differentiate simple and complex search objectives (Rouet, 1991). In other words, reading a hypertext requires some learning, but practice may be enough for simple hypertext systems. However, more elaborate training plans might be necessary when learning to use sophisticated systems. Finally, the issue of how hypertext skills may transfer back to traditional text formats (i.e., whether students might improve their reading skills by using hypertext) is of key importance, but it has received little attention so far.

SUMMARY AND CONCLUSION

In this chapter, we have presented some of the cognitive issues in the use of hypertext. We have suggested that a basic problem is the lack of a theoretical model to account for how people read and learn from nonlinear text. Analogies (e.g., reading as navigation) and metaphors (hypertext as an information space) are useful to a certain extent, but there is a strong need for more analytical approaches. The Cognitive Flexibility Theory (Spiro et al., 1988, 1991) is an example of such an approach.

The concept of nonlinearity is often misunderstood and wrongly associated with electronic text only. We have illustrated how nonlinear features can be embedded into linear text (i.e., online definitions). A few experiments have shown that introducing these "shallow" nonlinear features into electronic text can actually improve text comprehension. Computerized text provides less disruptive ways to access extra information and thus decreases the cognitive cost of this activity.

It is still debated whether real nonlinear texts, such as text networks, can support text learning. Several empirical studies have shown that reading a nonlinear text is a complex activity. Inexperienced users face important orientation and navigation difficulties. However, providing structure and coherence cues helps overcome these difficulties.

In light of these facts, we suggest that hypertext efficiency involves a trade-off between the power of the linking and search tools it provides and the cognitive demands or costs these tools impose on the reader. The power / cost ratio can be improved in two major ways; first, by providing structural cues that make hypertext look like the traditional text structures readers usually rely on, and second, by improving the readers' hypertext literacy, that is by helping readers become "hyper-readers," or experts in the use of nonlinear text.

Finally, we have to acknowledge that the study of the potential of hypertext for learning and instruction is still in its infancy. We believe that the studies and commentaries presented in this chapter are representative of the state of the art in hypertext research: A few interesting phenomena have been established, but a comprehensive conceptual framework is still missing. Further theoretical and empirical research studies on the issues of hypertext and cognition is a key step in the design of efficient information technology.

ACKNOWLEDGMENTS

Research presented in this chapter was supported in part by a University of Pittsburgh postdoctoral fellowship to the first author and by an ASLA-Fullbright research grant and Finnish Cultural Fund grant to the second author. The authors wish to thank Gareth Gabrys for his useful comments on an earlier version of this chapter.

REFERENCES

Bernstein, M., Joyce, M., & Levine, D. Contours of constructive hypertexts. In D. Lucarella, J. Nanard, & P. Paolini (Eds.), *Proceedings of the Fourth ACM Conference on Hypertext* (pp. 161–170). New York: ACM Press.

Black, A., Wright, P., Black, D., & Norman, K. (1992). Consulting on-line dictionary information while reading. *Hypermedia, 4*(3), 145–169.

Brown, P. J. (1992). UNIX Guide: Lessons from ten years' development. In D. Lucarella, J. Nanard, M. Nanard, & P. Paolini (Eds.), *ECHT'92: Proceedings of the Fourth ACM Conference on Hypertext* (pp. 63–70). New York: ACM Press.

Bush, V. (1945). As we may think. *Atlantic Monthly, 176*(1), July, 101–108.

Dee-Lucas, D., & Larkin, J. H. (1992). *Text representation with traditional text and hypertext* (Tech. Rep. H.P. #21). Pittsburgh: Carnegie Mellon University, Department of Psychology.

Dillon, A., McKnight, C., & Richardson, J. (1990). Navigation in hypertext: A critical review of the concept. In D. Diaper, D. Gilmore, G. Cockton, & B. Shackel (Eds.), *Proceedings of IFIP INTERACT '90: Human-computer interaction* (pp. 587–592). Amsterdam: Elsevier.

Dillon, A., McKnight, C., & Richardson, J. (1993). Space—the Final Chapter or why physical representations are not semantic intentions. In C. McKnight, A. Dillon, & J. Richardson (Eds.), *Hypertext: A psychological perspective* (pp. 169–191). Chichester, England: Ellis Horwood.

Dillon, A., Richardson, J., & McKnight, C. (1989). Human factors of journal usage and design of electronic texts. *Interacting with Computers, 1*(2), 183–189.

Duchastel, P. (1986). Intelligent computer-assisted instruction systems: The nature of learner control. *Journal of Educational Computing Research, 2*(5), 379–393.

Edwards, D., & Hardman, L. (1989). "Lost in hyperspace": Cognitive mapping and navigation in a hypertext environment. In R. McAleese (Ed.), *Hypertext: Theory into practice* (pp. 105–125). Oxford, England: Intellect.

Espéret, E. (1992). Hypertext processing: Can we forget textual psycholinguistics? In A. M. Oliveira (Ed.), *Structure of communication and intelligent helps for hypermedia courseware* (pp. 112–119). New York: Springer-Verlag.

Foltz, P. (1992). *Readers' comprehension and strategies in linear text and hypertext* (Technical Report No. 93.01). Boulder, CO: Institute of Cognitive Science.

Foss, C. L. (1989). *Detecting lost users: Empirical studies on browsing hypertext* (INRIA Technical Report No. 972, Programme 8). Sophia–Antipolis, France: INRIA.

Garner, R. (1987). Strategies for reading and studying expository text. *Educational Psychologist, 22*, 299–312.

Gordon, S., Gustavel, J., Moore, J., & Hankey, J. (1988). The effect of hypertext on reader knowledge representation. *Proceedings of the 32nd Annual Meeting of the Human Factors Society* (pp. 296–300). Santa Monica, CA: Human Factors Society.

Gray, S. H. (1990). Using protocol analysis and drawing to study mental model construction during hypertext navigation. *International Journal of Human-Computer Interaction, 2*(4), 359–377.

Gray, S. H., & Shasha, D. (1989). To link or not to link? Empirical guidance for the design of nonlinear text systems. *Behavior Research, Methods, Instruments and Computers, 21*(2), 326–333.

Happ, A. J., & Stanners, S. L. (1991). Effect of hypertext cue on knowledge representation. *Proceedings of the Human Factors Society 35th annual meeting,* issue no., pp. 305–309. Santa Monica, CA: Human Factors Society.

Jacobson, M. J., & Spiro, R. J. (1991). Hypertext learning environments and cognitive flexibility: Characteristics promoting the transfer of complex knowledge. In L. Birnbaum (Ed.), *Proceedings of the International Conference on the Learning Sciences* (pp. 240–248). Charlottesville, VA: Association for the Advancement of Computing in Education.

Lachman, R. (1989). Comprehension aids for online reading of expository text. *Human Factors, 31*(1), 1–15.

Landow, G. (1991). The status of the navigation problem. In R. Furuta & D. Stotts (Eds.), *Proceedings of the Third ACM Conference on Hypertext* (p. 364). New York: ACM Press.

Lehtinen, E., Balcytiene, A., & Gustafsson, M. (1993). *Knowledge structures, activity, and hypertext.* Paper presented at the Fifth European Conference for Research on Learning and Instruction. Aix-en-Provence, France.

Mayer, R. E. (1984). Aids to text comprehension. *Educational Psychologist, 19*(1), 30–42.

McKnight, C., Dillon, A., & Richardson, J. (1990). A comparison of linear and hypertext formats in information retrieval. In R. McAleese & C. Green (Eds.), *Hypertext: The state of art* (pp. 10–19). Oxford, England: Intellect Books.

Mohageg, M. F. (1992). The influence of hypertext linking structures on the efficiency of information retrieval. *Human Factors, 34*(3), 351–367.

Rada, R., & Murphy C. (1992). Searching versus browsing in hypertext. *Hypermedia, 4*(1), 1–31.

Reinking, D., & Rickman, S. S. (1990). The effects of computer-mediated text on the vocabulary learning and comprehension of intermediate grade readers. *Journal of Reading Behavior, 12*(4), 395–411.

Rouet, J.-F. (1990). Interactive text processing by inexperienced (hyper-) readers. In A. Rizk, N. Streitz, & J. André (Eds.), *Hypertexts: Concepts, systems, and applications* (pp. 250–260). Cambridge, England: Cambridge University Press.

Rouet, J.-F. (1991, December). *Learning to read a hypertext: A cognitive approach.* Poster presented at the Hypertext'91 conference, San Antonio, TX.

Rouet, J.-F. (1992). Cognitive processing of hyperdocuments: When does nonlinearity help? In D. Lucarella, J. Nanard, M. Nanard, & P. Paolini, *Proceedings of the 4th ACM Conference on Hypertext* (pp. 131–140). New York: ACM Press.

Rouet, J.-F., Britt, M. A., Mason, R. A., & Perfetti, C. A. (1992, November-December). *The use of hypertext system to study and reason about historical documents.* Poster presented at ECHT'92, 4th ACM conference on hypertext. Milan, Italy.

Schuler, W., & Smith, J. B. (1990). Author's argumentation assistant (AAA): A hypertext-based authoring tool for argumentative texts. In A. Rizk, N. Streitz, & J. André (Eds.) *Hypertext: Concepts, Systems and Applications* (pp. 137–151). Cambridge, England: Cambridge University Press.

Simpson, A., & McKnight, C. (1990). Navigation in hypertext: Structural cues and mental maps. In R. McAleese & C. Green (Eds.), *Hypertext: The state of the art* (pp. 74–83). Oxford, England: Intellect Books Ltd.

Smeaton, A. (1991). Using hypertext for computer based learning. *Computers in Education, 17*(3), 173–179.

Spiro, R. J. (1993, September). *Hypertext and cognitive flexibility: Towards a theory of nonlinear learning and instruction.* Paper presented at the 5th EARLI Conference. Aix-en-Provence, France.

Spiro, R. J., Coulson, R. L., Feltovich, P. J., & Anderson, D. K. (1988). Cognitive flexibility theory: Advanced knowledge acquisition in ill-structured domains. In *Proceedings of the Tenth Annual Conference of the Cognitive Science Society* (pp. 375–383). Hillsdale, NJ: Lawrence Erlbaum Associates.

Spiro, R. J., Feltovitch, P. J., Jacobson M. J., & Coulson, R. J. (1991). Cognitive flexibility, constructivism and hypertext: Random access instruction for advanced knowledge acquisition in ill-structured domains. *Educational Technology, 31*(5), 24–33.

Spyridakis, J. H., & Standal, T. C. (1987). Signals in expository prose: Effects on reading. *Reading Research Quarterly, 22*, 285–298.

Streitz, N., Hanneman, J., & Thüring, M. (1989). From ideas and arguments to hyperdocuments: Travelling through activity spaces. *Proceedings of ACM Hypertext '89* (pp. 343–364). New York: ACM Press.

Toulmin, S. (1958). *The uses of argument.* Cambridge, England: Cambridge University Press.

Tripp, S. D., & Robby, W. (1990). Orientation and disorientation in a hypertext lexicon. *Journal of Computer-Based Instruction, 17*(4), 120–124.

van Dijk, T. A., & Kintsch, W. (1983). *Strategies of discourse comprehension.* Hillsdale, NJ: Lawrence Erlbaum Associates.

Weyer, S. A. (1982). The design of a dynamic book for information search. *International Journal of Man-Machine Studies, 17*, 87–107.

Wright, P. (1991). Cognitive overheads and prostheses: Some issues in evaluating hypertexts. In R. Furuta & D. Stotts (Eds.), *Proceedings of the third ACM Conference on Hypertext* (pp. 1–12). New York: ACM Press.

3

▼▼▼▼▼▼▼

Myths, Misconceptions, and an Alternative Perspective on Information Usage and the Electronic Medium

Andrew Dillon
Indiana University

"Liberation of the reader," "an information revolution," and "freedom from constraints" are just three of the catch phrases that are bandied about with immodest regularity when talk amongst many educators, computer scientists, and even some psychologists turns to hypertext and its application to education (see e.g., Barrett, 1988; Beeman et al., 1987). In a world of increasing chip speeds and decreasing software costs, the computer provides us with both the image of ourselves as information processors and the potential for our salvation. This is heady stuff indeed.

The beauty of these perspectives is that you can buy into one and dismiss the other, and either way, you will still be eligible for membership of the technocrat club, that exclusive band of late 20th century scholars who claim to have seen the light (and know it flickers when active). Many cognitive scientists accept the computer metaphor of mind so uncritically that it is inconceivable for them that mental life does not flow through buffers and circuits in an algorithmic embrace of the biological hardware (see e.g., Johnson-Laird, 1988). Yet, these people may find little in common with others, often educationalists (Cunningham, Duffy, & Knuth, 1993), who are dismissive of such artifactual philosophizing. Putatively pragmatic, educationalists prefer applications of technology and want learning environments to be virtual, networked, and nonlinear, and every child to have a mouse, a menu, and a math coprocessor.

But what of the rest of us; those people who feel affinity with neither perspective, who see the computer for what it is—a potentially powerful tool when well designed and a dull collection of plastic and electronic circuits when not; no more, no less? What of those who view the impact and uptake of technology as both influenced by and influencing the social structures in which it is embedded? We seem banished to an intellectual no-man's land, somewhere between cognitive science and constructivism, labeled "luddite" at best and "technophobic" at worst. Our only sins are to question the computer metaphor of mind and to seek some evidence of the technology's impact on education that meets minimal standards of scientific rationality.

What I attempt to describe in this chapter is an alternative to the new technocracy that avoids technophobia and seeks to demonstrate that it is possible to be enthusiastic about new technologies without losing perspective of their true role, which is the service of humans.

HYPERTEXT AND THE INFORMATION REVOLUTION

It is generally assumed, but rarely demonstrated, by advocates of hypertext that humans are constrained by the supposedly inherent linear qualities of paper and forced to access and use information in a strongly directed fashion (Collier, 1987; Jonassen, 1989b). In the world of hypertext, this is seen as a bad thing. Hypertext is thus proposed as a superior presentation medium which can support more natural interactions with a variety of information sources. This idea can be traced back to Bush (1945) with his emphasis on the role of association in cognition, but although less explicitly associationist, current emphasis still focuses on the limitations of paper and the potential benefits of electronic documents (Nielsen, 1990).

In recent years, however, the glib predictions about the death of paper, the emergence of a paperless world, and the unmistakable advantages of hypertext have rung hollow. It was Jonassen (1982) who said, "in a decade or so, the book as we know it will be as obsolete as is movable type today" (p. 379), and Ted Nelson (1987) who argued, "the question is not can we do everything on screens, but when will we, how will we and how can we make it great? This is an article of faith—its simple obviousness defies argument."

Yet, the last decade of empirical evidence suggests that this article of faith, like most religious beliefs, does not defy argument. Research has shown that reading from screens is frequently slower (Gould et al., 1987), less accurate (Wilkinson & Robinshaw, 1987), and more fatiguing (Cushman, 1986). Because hypertext has generally failed to show the significant benefits in reading performance and learning that many predicted, few researchers are now willing to make the sweeping statements of the medium's earlier advocates (for a review of empirical findings on reading from paper and screen, see Dillon, 1992).

Furthermore, paper shows no signs of dying out as a result of this revolutionary new medium. Girill and Luk (1983) produced evidence more than 10 years ago to the effect that for every one line of text read on screen, over 100 lines were printed out, and this had dropped to a 1:17 ratio 3 years later (Girill, Luk, &

Norton, 1987). But even as the ratio dropped, the total amount of paper printed out increased. It should be seen as cautionary to those predicting a paperless world; the most successful applications of information technology to date have been the word processor, the fax, and the photocopier—technologies that provide everyone with the power to produce limitless amounts of paper at the push of a button!

Interestingly, such poor predictive ability concerning the impact of new technology should not surprise us. Scientists, technologists, and business analysts have a weak track record in predicting the social impact of new tools. McKnight, Dillon, and Richardson (1991) remarked that over time, innumerable artifacts have been predicted to change society including such unusual ones as the hosepipe and the beret. Humans absorb technological innovation at a pace that suits them, rejecting some and invariably putting others to only partial use. In so doing, they exploit technology in ways often unforeseen by the experts or the designers, rendering accurate predictions of impact difficult.

As a human factors professional or ergonomist, my interest in hypertext reflects a concern with the design of acceptable technology in general, and the analysis of human information usage in particular. By acceptable, I draw on Shackel's (1991) definition of acceptable technology as one which satisfies specific criteria for functionality, usability, and cost. Theoretical perspectives are undoubtedly enriching and essential for the long-term progress of the field, but, ultimately, empirical evidence is required both to bring about changes in contemporary design contexts and to introduce greater rationality into discussions of such technologies (Landauer, 1991). Far too often, the theoretical underpinnings of hypertext design spring from cognitive science or educational psychology with little alteration, as if such theoretical models could jump the theory–practice gap without difficulty. Yet, it has become clear over the last decade of research in the field of Human–Computer Interaction (HCI) that transferring social and cognitive science findings to design practice is rarely such a straightforward process (see e.g., Klein & Eason, 1991).

As a result, even in the absence of supporting evidence, the practice of hypertext design has been accompanied by an uncritical acceptance of a host of quasi-psychological notions of reading and cognition. Taken from the laboratory and applied to the everyday context of reading, such theories become diluted and misunderstood. Rather than using the real world as a shaper of theory, contemporary hypertext thinking seems tied to concepts of association and non-linearity of access even as it distorts them. Such issues are of importance because our theories of information use and human cognition are themselves shapers of future technologies.

Several myths and misconceptions about reading permeate the hypertext design world and need to be corrected if progress is to be made in this field. I examine these myths in turn, drawing on evidence in support of my points. I attempt to show that hypertext has largely failed to fulfill much of its early promise, and that this should not surprise us as, in reality, the *Zeitgeist* is currently techno-centric, despite expressed concern for users. That is, the very term "user centered" is in danger of becoming clichéd and it is used regularly in the absence of any genuine attempt to understand users (see Dillon, Sweeney, & Maguire, 1993b, for evidence). Furthermore, I contend that current design thinking is always prone to confuse capability in technological terms with acceptability in human terms. As a result of numerous empirical examinations of readers' verbal protocols and performance with a variety of documents, paper, and hypertext, a framework for the evaluation of hypertext applications is proposed which emphasizes usability as the major test for new technologies.

Myth 1: Associative Linking of Information Is Natural in That It Mimics the Workings of the Human Mind

Virtually all introductory writings on hypertext make reference to the notion of association and nonlinearity and there is little to be gained by rehashing the arguments here (Nielsen, 1995). What is important, however, is both the belief that the association of information deemed possible with hypertext is somehow more natural to users (as readers or learners) than paper presentations of the same information, and the effects that this belief has on subsequent designs.

Naturalistic associationism as manifest in the hypertext literature holds that knowledge is represented cognitively in some form of semantic network or web. The exact form, however, is rarely precisely stated and terms such as schemata and networks, scripts, and webs are employed by writers on the subject with little or no recourse to contemporary psychological developments (Jonassen, 1993). Anderson's ACT* framework enables an associative view of cognition but is formally distinguished by researchers in the field of cognitive science from schema theory (Anderson, 1983). This is not to say that ACT* is to be favored over schema theory in hypertext design, but it does mean that in drawing on such theories, one is at least appreciative of these differences. Without such clarity, conceptual confusion occurs and progress through theory building is handicapped as people use terms in a subjective manner and claim theoretical support from inappropriate quarters.

Unfortunately, such distinctions in the cognitive science literature appear to have minimal impact on writers in the hypertext field. This has resulted in a literature replete with theoretically dubious statements of the following kind: "The practice of 'associative linking' and re-centering may be the best approximation of how a trained mind approaches a problem" (Delany & Gilbert, 1991, p. 290), or "Schema theory contends that knowledge is stored in information packets or schemas that comprise our mental constructs for ideas. Schemas have attributes, which most often consist of other schemas" (Jonassen, 1993, pp. 153–154).

The inevitable result in contemporary writing on this subject is theoretical confusion and the rationalization of design decisions on superficial or weakly articulated cognitive perspectives. In terms of linking and associating information nodes, it has resulted in a pervasive sense of serving the user or learner simply by putting information into a system and enabling it all to be linked.

Even if the claims for hypertext are perhaps now couched less explicitly in terms of the "natural" relationship between cognition and nonlinear information structures, they are still made implicitly by many educators who believe that the technology offers the potential for greater or richer learning experience than paper artifacts (see e.g., Small & Grabowski, 1992, for a contemporary example). Indeed, Jonassen (1989a) explicitly argued that hypertext could be effective for the very reason that it could represent a model of the expert's knowledge structure and content which should be acquired by the learner.

This is to my mind an unsubstantiated (and perhaps even untestable) claim. The representation of the information or knowledge, and these terms are really not synonymous, is only one aspect of providing a learning environment. As has been argued elsewhere (Dillon, Richardson, & McKnight, 1993a), a learner may be able to reproduce the teacher's knowledge representation as manifest in both hypertext and paper forms, but this is no guarantee of meaningful learning having occurred. Certainly, Jonassen's (1993) most recent empirical attempts at demonstrating the value of modeling experts' knowledge structures with hypertext failed to produce any desired effects, leading him to conclude that hypertext might not be an appropriate mechanism for supporting some learning tasks after all.

The semantic intention of the author is very different from the physical representation of the text or graphic on screen and if one really could convey meaning and organization in the knowledge sense merely by reorganizing the layout of the physical page or screen to highlight associations, then we would have far fewer learning problems to worry about. Unfortunately, it is not that simple and the best efforts of researchers to date have failed to provide us with well-documented examples of enhanced learning through hypertext (see for example Rouet and Levonen, in this volume, for a detailed discussion of the problems here).

Myth 2: Paper Is a Linear and Therefore a Constraining Medium

Hypertext advocates portray paper as a limiting medium, claiming it imposes a "linear straitjacket of ink on paper" (Collier, 1987). This is usually contrasted with the much vaunted liberating characteristics of hypertext, which, with its basic form of nodes and links, is seen to be somehow freer or more natural. Nielsen (1995), for example, reflected the consensus view with the following summary: "All traditional text . . . is sequential, meaning that there is a single linear sequence defining the order in which it is to be read. First you read page one. Then you read page two. Then you read page three . . . Whereas hypertext is nonsequential; there is no single order in which the text is to be read" (p. 1).

Similar and even more extreme positions can be found in many of the writings describing the claimed wonders of hypertext (Delaney & Landow, 1991; Nelson, 1987).

Such views do not provide a fair representation of paper or of hypertext, for that matter. Certainly, reading a sentence is largely a linear activity, although eye movement data suggest that even here, some nonlinearity does occur (Just & Carpenter, 1980). Therefore, on screen, reading text is still as likely to be predominantly linear, at least at paragraph and sentence levels. The issue then is the extent to which linearity is imposed on the reader at the multisentence level in using the document.

Though paper texts may be said to have a physical linear format, there is little evidence to suggest that readers are constrained by this or that they only read such texts in a straightforward start-to-finish manner (Charney, 1987; Horney, 1993; Pugh, 1979). For example, in an examination of academic journal usage, Dillon, Richardson, and McKnight (1989) identified three reading strategies, only one of which could be described as linear; the other two involved rapid browsing and jumping throughout the text depending on the task goal at the time (check references, get a feel for the contents, identify statistical analysis, etc.), for which the established structure of the text under discussion enabled multiple nonlinear moves on the part of the reader. Further evidence to contradict the idea of constrained linear access can be found in a similar analysis of software manual usage (Dillon, 1991a).

With hypertext, movement might involve less physical manipulation (a mouse movement, for example, compared to turning and folding pages) or less cognitive effort (a selectable link to information compared to looking up an index and then manipulating the text), but these are matters of degree, not of category. We must be clear on this point or face accusations of distortion in our arguments. One could make a case for paper being the liberator as at least the reader always has access to the full text, even if searching it might prove awkward. With hypertext, the absence of links could deny some readers access to information and force them to follow someone else's ideas of where the information trail should lead.

In many ways, this is little more than common sense; we knew this all along. However, the myth of paper's linearity has taken hold in the field despite the evidence from researchers in related disciplines such as text linguistics (de Beaugrande, 1980) and textbook design (Whalley, 1993), that authors normally seek to convey their argument in text by utilizing a range of structural elements that are not constrained by linearity of delivery and uptake (e.g., core and adjunct text forms). Furthermore, recent evidence (Dillon, 1991b) indicates that experienced readers of paper documents have expectations of organization within documents that they use to guide manipulation and location in precisely such nonlinear manners. In accepting too uncritically the myth, many hypertext developments seem more concerned with superficial presentational details than with formal analysis of information presentation and processing.

An argument could be made for the effect of experience here. The typical readers of the text types just cited were frequent, skilled readers of such texts and might have developed such reading strategies despite the much-claimed restriction of the paper medium. I would counter this with two arguments.

First, evidence has been provided that even when faced with a unique text form, typical readers respond by employing such strategies. McKnight, Dillon, and Richardson (1990) created a paper version of a document that had only previously been available on hypertext, and reported that even with no prior exposure to it, readers demonstrably accessed the material in a nonlinear form. For sure, the readers in their experiment seemed to manifest more serial reading of sections, but not one of them read the text in the simple start-to-finish manner we would expect to observe if they had been constrained by this medium.

Second, if hypertext is seen to be more liberating only for the readers or learners who are exposed to it at the earliest possible stages in their reading development, then of course, one can explain away the evidence McKnight et al. (1990) provided. However, in so doing, we move from a claim for hypertext as liberating for typical readers (the usual claim) to one where we advocate it as most suitable for the beginning reader. This is a very different claim, one which is rarely articulated in the literature and furthermore one that is likely to find little support given its logical implication for most users of current technologies.

Myth 3: Rapid Access to a Large Manipulable Mass of Information Will Lead to Better Use and Learning

The belief that enabling access to and manipulation of masses of information in an obviously nonlinear manner is desirable and will somehow increase learning (however measured) is ever present in discussions on educational hypertext. Ambron (1988), for example, claimed that with hypertext one can browse, annotate, link, and elaborate information to explore and integrate vast libraries of multimedia information, an argument echoed by Megarry (1988) who also emphasized the potential to explore knowledge with hypertext.

How will this be achieved, however? Since when did exploration of information inevitably lead to integration, particularly with large amounts of information? And can we really talk about exploring libraries of knowledge? Claims for "learner empowerment" (Small & Grabowski, 1992) have been made without critical evidence that it is needed, is possible, or even works. The analysis of hypertext usage makes great play of the medium's potential, but rarely demonstrates objectively how this is achieved. Furthermore, as Hammond (1993) asked, how many learning scenarios really require such free-ranging interactions over large amounts of information?

To date, the claims have far exceeded the evidence and few hypertext systems have been shown to lead to either greater comprehension or significantly better performance levels. Clearly, mere exposure to information is not enough for learning to occur, which we really always knew.[1] And where the medium fails to produce the effect that was required, too little emphasis is placed on relating the assumptions behind the design of the information presentation medium to the psychological activities of the learner. This concern with vast information sources over real human needs betrays the technocentric values of its proponents even while they talk in user-centered terms.

Years of educational research have attempted to design teaching systems, from Skinnerian programmed learning machines to constructivist technology. Furthermore, systems design is not essentially an educational issue but an informational one, and this distinction is all too rarely made in the hypertext community. As I argued elsewhere (Dillon 1994), the artifacts we create are instantiations of our theories of the user. If these theories are based on naive assumptions (e.g., the human mind works by association or paper forces people to read linearly), then it is only logical that the resulting technologies are unlikely to prove acceptable. I would endorse iterative design in the search for better artifacts, but with the prerequisite that we articulate clearly the theories of the user that are driving them and seek to test their assumptions in order to improve such theories.

Myth 4: Future Technologies Will Solve All Current Problems

Visions of paperless worlds and virtual libraries collapse relatively quickly when one experiences the reality of most HyperCard applications or Guide documents. This myth of a bright future is really little more than the dogma of technological determinism. Yet, it turns up continually in writings on this new medium (see e.g., Delany & Landow, 1991). The vision of the future is always unbearably bright and the resulting loss of clarity is a natural consequence of such ill-informed imaginings. It is not even the case that new technologies have just produced new problems; they have, but have often failed to solve the old ones too.

Hypertext versions of academic literature have been examined with some success (McKnight et al., 1991). But the problems of increasing learning with advanced technology remain and we are no nearer to solving the problems of computer assisted learning with hypertext than we were with previous technologies. Furthermore, as long as we rely on educational theory or technocratic speculation alone, little progress appears possible.

---

[1]Witness what I shall term here, the "Maastricht phenomenon." Maastricht, a small Dutch town, was the name given to a treaty among states in the European community. Recent reports show that more than 9 million words were written on this treaty over the last 12 months in the English press. Yet, when asked "what is Maastricht?" most British citizens, who claimed to read newspapers, could not say! However, ever willing, some members of the public proffered their views. Some of the more interesting answers suggested Maastricht was either a sexually transmitted disease or "something to do with the ozone layer."

An Alternative Perspective

Four myths have been examined and four myths have been found wanting. The new technology is neither naturally like us nor certain to lead to educational improvements. So where do we start if we want an alternative take on hypertext and do not wish to fall pray to technophobia?

From an ergonomic or human factors perspective,[2] designing hypertext systems is no different from designing any other interactive technology and therefore, consideration in the first instance must be given to the learning task and to users as learners. But what is the task in learning? Clearly, there can be no broad task that constitutes learning in all its manifestations. Learning is a complex, multidetermined activity or process that cannot just be equated with information retrieval, target location, navigation, or memorization alone.

In human factors terms, learning would be viewed as the user's goal for which technology offers partial support, just as "getting work done" or "performing a job" are viewed as human goals beyond the level of interaction with a computer. These would be considered too high a level of analysis or description for artifact evaluation, and of necessity, would be divided into what are termed "tasks." It should be noted that tasks in turn can be subdivided into "acts" and the complete set of tasks a person performs is called their "job." Indeed, it is rare to find mention of any such system goal in the ergonomics literature (i.e., "the system is designed to enhance learning") except in broad initial discussions of the design.

In this sense, learning, as a goal (or job, work, etc.) needs to be addressed at a task level where, indeed, aspects of information location, summarization of ideas, memory, and so forth, may be identified. Such tasks can be analyzed and subsequently supported technologically. In so designing the technological support (hypertextual or otherwise), empirical methods can be employed to determine usability and to assess the extent to which the technology increases learner performance on that task (though this is usually a different issue from whether or not learning was being supported). Clearly, the analysis of real-world information usage and learning tasks would at least raise questions about the myths of hypertext outlined previously.

Empirical work on hypertext is in short supply, yet it is our best hope of progress in this field. What is salutary is that attempts at designing demonstrably effective hypertext systems (i.e., those satisfying the empirical test criterion) have needed to rely heavily on user testing to ensure even partial success. The SuperBook project at Bellcore (Landauer et al., 1993) is a case in point. Although

---

[2]The term ergonomics refers to the multidisciplinary study of humans in working environments, with particular emphasis on the design of technology to support human performance. In the United States, this work is more often termed human factors, although a shift is occurring toward a more general acceptance of the European term. In some sense, neither term is particularly satisfactory in describing the perspective outlined here, which necessarily embraces some perspectives from information science and possibly from instructional design.

SuperBook is commonly cited (justifiably) as a hypertext success story, it is important to realize that the early developments of SuperBook actually led to significantly poorer user performance relative to paper in certain tasks.

Although Landauer et al. managed to redesign the hypertext effectively, they admitted to being able to do so only on the basis of empirical data that had highlighted substantial delays at certain task points due to poor system response rate and had shown users to be employing suboptimal search strategies. Even modifying the first version successfully still left room for further improvement as subsequent evaluations indicated other sources of user difficulty.

Similarly, McKnight et al. (1992) designed a system following user-centered methods. On observing equivalent comprehension levels between this medium and a paper equivalent among university students, they claimed their design to be a success. Given the then existing evidence in the field, such a claim had some credence. That experiment tested matched groups of students using either 40,000 word hypertext or paper as a resource for gathering material in order to produce an essay on an issue in a general area in which they had received prior instruction—a typical educational activity. The resulting essays were scored by an expert examiner in the field using a clearly articulated evaluation procedure, again much like a typical university-level examination.

Neither of these studies started from any detailed theoretical assumption about the learner, and neither made any claims for learner empowerment, but concentrated first and foremost on task-based empirical methods. Furthermore, neither group claimed on the basis of their results that anything had been demonstrated about learning per se. McKnight et al. (1992), for example, concluded explicitly that they had only demonstrated in this situation that hypertext could lead to comprehension levels equivalent to paper. No learning theory was invoked or required to understand the results. More importantly, the notion of using this technology in educational contexts is deemed a problem for analysis at a different level of discourse, one predicated on curriculum design, teaching methods, and learning assessment, rather than usability.

What such studies do highlight is the importance of task and user variables as well as the need to analyze the process of interaction in order to produce effective performance outcomes on a range of information usage tasks. The SuperBook project followed a classic user-centered design process, but it points to several difficulties hypertext interface designers face in educational environments. First, empirical trials are expensive. Even where cheap prototypes can be utilized, locating and training representative users for evaluation purposes and analyzing the subsequent data is not cheap and thus, is frequently resisted by design teams. Second, the problems identified in the user trials for SuperBook were not complex (e.g., response rate, poorly formulated search criteria, etc.). With hindsight, these problems seem obvious, and there is certainly an established literature on the effect of such variables on human performance with computers, yet none of this highly talented design team predicted them. This is the norm and will occur in all design processes until we have theories of the user or learner that can predict such responses to the interface.

The McKnight et al. (1992) work demonstrates the importance of under-standing a particular learning task and of creating a hypertext environment that matches the learners' needs and expectations of information structure. These needs and expectations were elicited through interviews with potential users. Readers have expectations of structure in a range of paper document types, and removing these in some misguided attempt at liberating the reader is likely to prove detrimental to usage. Furthermore, the design of this hypertext application took on board the relevant design findings on interface variables and user performance (e.g., screen size, image polarity, manipulation facilities), demon-strating the applicability of this work to design practice.

By conceptualizing the technology rightly as a support element of the learning environment and by placing emphasis on ensuring usability from the learner's perspective, ergonomic analysis enables education to proceed along appropriate lines where the learner, the educator, and the technology (or learning environment) form a work or educational system. The designing of the technology forms just one important part of the total system and it is not necessarily one that requires or is even well-served by an educational theory. However, although this perspec-tive casts doubt on many of the beliefs surrounding hypertext and education that are in vogue, it also suggests that the design of usable pedagogic environments is a theoretically impoverished area. User-centered design philosophies are rarely methods and the need for data-driven design remains with us for all interactive tools. In the following section, a framework is proposed to help the design team think about hypertext in a user-centered (and nonmythical) fashion at the earliest stages, hopefully ensuring better quality prototyping and evaluation planning, and thereby lessening the risk of gathering data on usability that disappoints or fails to inform redesign.

A FRAMEWORK OF READER–DOCUMENT INTERACTION

Over the course of several long-term projects, readers' and learners' interactions with documents have been studied. The documents studied have been both paper and electronic (including a range of hypertext forms), and of several types (aca-demic, professional, technical, etc.). In the course of such work (see McKnight et al., 1991; Dillon, 1994) I have studied readers' behavior and concurrent verbal protocols while using documents to perform numerous tasks. This work has led to the proposal of the following descriptive framework. The framework (known as TIMS for Tasks, Information model, Manipulation facilities, and Standard reading) is intended to be an approximate representation of the human cognition and behavior central to the reading or information usage process. It consists of four interactive elements that reflect the primary components of reading at different phases. They are: A Task Model (T) that deals with the reader's needs and uses for the material; An Information Model (I) that provides a model of the information space; A set of manipulation skills and facilities (M) that support physical use of the material; and A Standard Reading Processor (S) that represents the cognitive and perceptual processing involved in reading words and sentences.

These are interrelated components reflecting the cognitive, perceptual, and psychomotor aspects of reading in any given context. According to this framework, document usage or reading is not a matter of merely scanning words on a page or of acquiring or applying a representational model of the text's structure, but a product of both these activities in conjunction with manipulating the document or information space and defining and achieving goals (all within a certain context). So, for example, a reader recognizes an information need, formulates a method of resolving this need, samples the document or information space appropriately applying her model of its structure and their task, manipulates it physically as required, and then perceives (in the experimental psychological sense) words on text until the necessary information is obtained.

Less serially, shifts may occur at all times between elements depending on one's purpose and on the variable determinants of information being gained (or not) such as altering one's reading goal in light of new information or modifying one's initial information models to take account of new experiences with the information space. The TIMS components are the building blocks of the activity described as reading or information usage that can be combined in numerous permutations. Each of these elements and their various interactions are described in more detail in Dillon (1994), but in the present chapter, I briefly outline how such a framework can aid our thinking on all matters hypertextual.

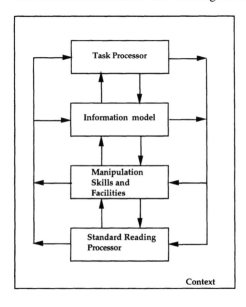

FIG. 3.1. The TIMS framework for describing human–text usage.

Applications of the Framework in the User-Centered Design of Hypertext

The framework is intended to support several uses. A designer (and I use the term here to include academics concerned with developing teaching materials as well as traditional software design teams) can use it simply as a checklist to ensure that all important components of the text under design are considered. This guards against the reliance on research findings at one level to ensure good design (e.g., just following the advice on visual ergonomics which concludes that certain fonts, polarity, and resolution variables can overcome the reading speed deficit). Although such advice might be pertinent and applicable, the framework suggests that it is but one part of the problem of designing usable hypertext.

Second, it could be used to guide design by allowing a designer to conceptualize the issues to be dealt with in advance of any specification or prototype. In this sense, it enables the hypertext designer to organize his or her thoughts on the problem and to highlight attributes of the specification that need to be considered. If this leads to significantly more appropriate first specifications or prototypes, lessening the number of iterations required and thereby reducing the time and costs involved in design, it will serve a particularly useful purpose.

Third, the framework supports the derivation of predictions about readers' performance with a document. Dillon (1994) highlighted its potential value as a predictive tool for a human factors practitioner, adequately familiar with the research in this area, to predict the type of problems a reader will face using an electronic document. The framework can support the derivation of predicted reading behavior through the analysis of the various elements and their manifestation or support in the relevant designs.

Finally, the framework has potential evaluative applications. It could be used to guide expert evaluation of a system under development (i.e., a usability assessment) and support troubleshooting for weaknesses in design. This proposed use is not unlike the first use outlined earlier except that it occurs at a different stage in the design process and is intended to support reasoned examination of the quality of an instantiated design. In this role, one could imagine a designer using the framework to check how the system rated on variables such as image quality, the information model it presents, the type of tasks it will support, or manipulations it enables.

A concrete example or two will draw these potential applications out more clearly. Consider a design team addressing the development of a new hypertext application to support the teaching of critical reading. Rather than buying into any of the myths that permeate the field, the TIMS framework would suggest analysis of the task first. Thus, the intended goal of the system (to support critical reading skill development) is reformulated operationally, for example, into comparing and contrasting sections of text by same or different authors. Once we have a clear idea of the nature of the users' interactions with the system, we can proceed to move through the other components of TIMS, examining in turn the likely information structures the users already possess for this text type, the constraints such structures might place on organizing or linking information, onto the best form of manipulation facilities required for such tasks, until finally we consider the ergonomic principles of screen design that affect reading text. All this can be performed in principle before a single line of code is produced (although in reality one would advocate rapid iterative prototyping on some of these issues) and could certainly lead to the identification of issues for which no good answer exists and thus, should be investigated further before design commitments are made.

At the other end of the design spectrum, we can consider an application of the framework in the evaluation stage. Despite the undoubted value of full field trials of new technology, the reality of most design scenarios requires that expert or heuristic evaluations be performed by a human factors specialist (or even by the designers). In this case, TIMS offers a cohesive framework from which to judge the ergonomic practicalities of a hypertext. It indicates that in any context of use, the evaluator needs to consider all four components of the framework in forming an opinion of an artifact's usability. Thus, it would be deemed insufficient merely to consider the screen ergonomics in terms of image quality or conformance to style guidelines, or to judge that for say, typical students, a mouse is a better manipulation device than function keys, and so forth. Instead, the evaluator is encouraged to consider task specifics such as how and why the application will be used, and the structure of the information in terms of its support for navigation. In making one's views on all components explicit, a more complete heuristic evaluation is enabled which at least touches on all issues that have been shown to affect user performance with a system.

Dillon (1994) has employed the framework in making explicit predictions about user performance in specific usage scenarios. For example, given two forms of accessing specific information (paper or hypertext), likely user behavior was described by tracing activities for the task through the TIMS components and indicating likely areas of advantage or disadvantage for either medium. The empirical results were a good fit to the predictions.

Thus, with such ergonomic perspectives, it is intended that designers are in a position to address basic design issues in their attempt to develop usable technological artifacts. No claims are made for hypertext with this perspective beyond those which have been empirically demonstrated, and the discussion of the user in this context makes no reference to association, exploration of vast knowledge stores, linearity, or nonlinearity. One could invoke them, but the use of TIMS neither depends on nor encourages such speculative discussion.

So Where Is the Learning?

Hypertext does, and will continue, to influence our creation and use of information. In that sense, it must have an impact on education and learning activities. However, it is still only a technology, and one that stores, manipulates, and presents information that could be presented in other ways. It may be more compact, support faster retrieval, allow greater manipulation, and so forth, but it is still an information presentation medium.

To believe that any new technology offers us the means of solving our educational problems is to buy into the new technocracy. This new technocracy is not really very different from the older technocracies of Skinner Boxes and CAL terminals (although its theoretical cohesion might certainly be weaker at this time). Yet, hypertext can play a part if designed and used appropriately. What I am arguing for here is a reorientation of our perspectives so that we proceed logically and to the best of our abilities. That means we do not equate learning with the simple process of interaction with a machine but see it as a process involving information access and use. In designing technology for such access and use, we do not need recourse to educational theory as it now stands but to the principles of ergonomics and user-centered systems design.

Educational theory subsequently plays a part in understanding what it is about the use of such well-designed machines that we can exploit in creating learning contexts where educators and students can exploit the technology's information handling and presentation qualities. The ergonomic and educational issues are located at different levels of analysis, but are intertwined when we seek to understand just what it is that hypertext may offer in pedagogical contexts. The onus is on developers of hypertext systems to produce a technology that supports users' learning tasks (clearly articulated in operational terms), emphasizing usability (the effectiveness, efficiency, and satisfaction of use according to emerging international standards for software: ISO 9241, Part 11) in the first instance rather than any increase in learning. Learning may be enhanced by certain technological inputs to the educational context, but only if the technological input is usable and not solely a result of that technology's presence but also of judicious use and careful support from the teacher or trainer. The latter issue is most appropriately addressed by educational theorists.

There is no need for educators or trainers to throw away established learning principles or teaching paradigms because of this. This is not to say that the established principles are right (indeed much of educational theory is particularly poor at predicting learning outcome), but the need for change should be empirically and ultimately theoretically determined. Our understanding of learning needs to develop on the basis of our experimental work and theoretical developments at the human rather than machine level. Furthermore, we must be clear that informing design with such theories and data requires more than just a simple cross-disciplinary reading of the literature. Bridging representations are required to enable such transfer. The framework described here is an attempt to provide one such bridge and to aid hypertext developers address the fundamental user issues appropriately before attempting any introduction of advanced technology to the learning context.

ACKNOWLEDGMENTS

I would like to thank my fellow editors, Dr. Peter Foltz of LRDC, Pittsburgh, and Professor Blaise Cronin of SLIS, Indiana University, for comments on earlier drafts that led to significant improvements in the present chapter.

REFERENCES

Ambron, S. (1988). What is multimedia? In S. Ambron & K. Hooper (Eds.), *Interactive multimedia.* Redmond, WA: Microsoft Press.

Anderson, J. (1983). *The architecture of cognition.* Cambridge, MA: Harvard University Press.

Barrett, E. (1988). *Text, context and hypertext.* Cambridge, MA: MIT Press.

Beeman, W., Anderson, K., Bader, G., Larkin, J., McClard, A., McQuillan, M., & Shields, M. (1987). Hypertext and pluralism: from lineal to non-lineal thinking. In *Proceedings of Hypertext '87* (pp. 67–88). Chapel Hill: University of North Carolina.

Bush, V. (1945). As we may think. *Atlantic Monthly, 176*(1), 101–108.

Charney, D. (1987). Comprehending non-linear text: The role of discourse cues. In *Proceedings of Hypertext '87* (pp. 109–120). Chapel Hill: University of North Carolina.

Collier, G. (1987). Thoth-II: Hypertext with explicit semantics. In *Proceedings of Hypertext '87* (pp. 269–289). Chapel Hill: University of North Carolina.

Cunningham, D., Duffy, T., & Knuth, R. (1993). The textbook of the future. In C. McKnight, A. Dillon, & J. Richardson (Eds.), *Hypertext: A psychological perspective* (pp. 19–50). Chichester, England: Ellis Horwood.

Cushman, W. H. (1986). Reading from microfiche, VDT and the printed page: Subjective fatigue and performance. *Human Factors, 28*(1), 63–73.

de Beaugrande, R. (1980). *Text, discourse and process.* Norwood, NJ: Ablex.

Delany, P., & Gilbert J. (1992). In P. Delaney & G. Landow (Eds.), *Hypertext and literary studies.* Cambridge, MA: MIT Press.

Delaney, P., & Landow, G. (Eds.). (1991). *Hypertext and literary studies.* Cambridge, MA: MIT Press.

Dillon, A. (1991a). Requirements analysis for hypertext applications: The why, what and how approach. *Applied Ergonomics, 22*(4), 458–462.

Dillon, A. (1991b). Readers' models of text structures: The case of academic articles. *International Journal of Man-Machine Studies, 35,* 913–925.

Dillon, A. (1992). Reading from paper versus screens: A critical review of the empirical literature. *Ergonomics: Third Special Issue on Cognitive Ergonomics, 35*(10), 1297–1326.

Dillon, A. (1994). *Designing usable electronic text: Ergonomics aspects of human information usage.* London: Taylor & Francis.

Dillon, A., Richardson, J., & McKnight, C. (1989). The human factors of journal usage and the design of electronic text. *Interacting with Computers, 1*(2), 183–189.

Dillon, A., Richardson, J., & McKnight, C. (1993a). Space—the final chapter: Or why physical representations are not semantic intentions. In C. McKnight, A. Dillon, & J. Richardson (Eds.), *Hypertext: A psychological perspective* (pp. 169–192). Chichester, England: Ellis Horwood.

Dillon, A., Sweeney, M., & Maguire, M. (1993b). A survey of usability evaluation practices and requirements in the European IT industry. In J. Alty, S. Guest, & D. Diaper (Eds.), *HCI'93: People and computers VII* (pp. 81–94). Cambridge, England: Cambridge University Press.

Girill, T., & Luk, C. (1983). Document: An interactive online solution of our documentation problems. *Communications of the ACM, 26*(5), 328–337.

Girill, T., Luk, C., & Norton, S. (1987). Reading patterns in online documentation: How transcript analysis reflects text design, software constraints and user preferences. In *Proceedings of 34th International Technical Communications Conference* (pp. 111–114). Washington, DC: STC.

Gould, J. D., Alfaro, L., Barnes, V., Finn, R., Grischkowsky, N., & Minuto, A. (1987). Reading is slower from CRT displays than from paper: Attempts to isolate a single variable explanation. *Human Factors, 29*(3), 269–299.

Hammond, N. (1993). Learning with hypertext: Problems, principles and prospects. In C. McKnight, A. Dillon, & J. Richardson (Eds.), *Hypertext: A psychological perspective* (pp. 51–70). Chichester, England: Ellis Horwood.

Horney, M. (1993). A measure of hypertext linearity. *Journal of Educational Multimedia and Hypermedia, 2*(1), 67–82.

Johnson-Laird, P. (1988). A computational analysis of sonciousness. In A. Marcel & E. Bisiach (Eds.), *Consciousness in contemporary science* (pp. 357–368). Oxford: Clarendon Press.

Jonassen, D. (1982). *The technology of text: Vol. I. Principles for structuring, designing, and displaying text.* Englewood Cliffs, NJ: Educational Technology Publications.

Jonassen, D. (1989a). Mapping the structure of content in instructional systems technology. *Educational Technology, 29*(4), 36–43.

Jonassen, D. (1989b). *Hypertext/hypermedia.* Englewood Cliffs, NJ: Educational Technology Publications.

Jonassen, D. (1993). Effects of semantically structured hypertext knowledge bases on users' knowledge structures. In C. McKnight, A. Dillon, & J. Richardson (Eds.), *Hypertext: A psychological perspective* (pp. 153–168). Chichester, England: Ellis Horwood.

Just, M. A., & Carpenter, P. (1980). A theory of reading: From eye movements to comprehension. *Psychological Review, 87*(4), 329–354.

Klein, L., & Eason, K. (1991). *Putting social science to work.* Cambridge, England: Cambridge University Press.

Landauer, T. (1991). Let's get real: A position paper on the role of cognitive psychology in the design of humanly useful and usable systems. In J. Carroll (Ed.), *Designing interaction: Psychology at the human-computer interface* (pp. 60–73). Cambridge, England: Cambridge University Press.

Landauer, T., Egan, D., Remde, J., Lesk, M., Lochbaum, C., & Ketchum, D. (1993). Enhancing the usability of text through computer delivery and formative evaluation. In C. McKnight, A. Dillon, & J. Richardson (Eds.), *Hypertext: A psychological perspective* (pp. 71–136). Chichester, England: Ellis Horwood.

McKnight, C., Dillon, A., & Richardson, J. (1990). A comparison of linear and hypertext formats in information retrieval. In R. McAleese & C. Green (Eds.), *Hypertext: State of the art* (pp. 10–19). Oxford, England: Intellect.

McKnight, C., Dillon, A., & Richardson, J. (1991). *Hypertext in context.* Cambridge, England: Cambridge University Press.

McKnight, C., Dillon, A., & Richardson, J. (1992). *Project CHIRO: Collaborative Hypertext in Research Organisations* (British Library Research Report). London: The British Library.

Megarry, J. (1988). Hypertext and compact disks. *British Journal of Educational Technology, 19*(3), 172–183.

Nelson, T. (1987). *Literary machines* (Abridged Electronic Version 87.1). San Antonio: Author.

Nielsen, J. (1995). Multimedia and hypertext: The Internet and beyond. Cambridge, MA: AP Professional.

Pugh, A. (1979). Styles and strategies in adult silent reading. In P. Kolers, M. Wrolstad, & H. Bouma (Eds.), *Processing of Visible Language 1* (pp. 308–317). London: Plenum Press.

Shackel, B. (1991). Usability-context, framework, definition, design and evaluation. In B. Shackel & S. Richardson (Eds.), *Human factors for informatics usability* (pp. 21–37). Cambridge, England: Cambridge University Press.

Small, R., & Grabowski, B. (1992). An exploratory study of information seeking behaviours and learning with hypermedia information systems. *Journal of Educational Multimedia and Hypermedia, 1*(4), 445–464.

Whalley, P. (1993). An alternative rhetoric for hypertext. In C. McKnight, A. Dillon, & J. Richardson (Eds.), *Hypertext: A psychological perspective* (pp. 7–18). Chichester, England: Ellis Horwood.

Wilkinson, R. T., & Robinshaw, H. M. (1987). Proof-reading: VDU and paper text compared for speed, accuracy and fatigue. *Behaviour and Information Technology, 6*(2), 125–133.

4

▼▼▼▼▼▼▼

Using Hypertext to Study and Reason About Historical Evidence

M. Anne Britt
Slippery Rock University

Jean-François Rouet
URA CRNC

Charles A. Perfetti
University of Pittsburgh

Suppose you want to learn what happened in 1903 to allow the United States to build a canal in Panama. You might start by reading a textbook excerpt to get the main events of the story and proceed from there to consult the supplied references. After getting these additional historians' accounts, you may also want to consult the specific documentary evidence they cite, such as treaties, letters, and speeches. Once you have all these documents, you would probably not merely read them in a serial, linear order. For instance, while reading one historian's account you may want to look back at what another historian said about that same event (especially if they contradict each other). Or you may want to develop your own interpretation of the evidence cited so you would read the cited document yourself and then reread the historian's evaluation of that document. This situation is a perfect one for the application of hypertext.

Learning and reasoning in history often necessitates the use of multiple interrelated documents. Although each document can be comprehended in isolation, a full understanding of the historical theme or problem requires the comparison and integration of various sources. Such complex textual analyses require the application of sophisticated study strategies (Anderson & Armbruster, 1984). For instance, in order to integrate information across multiple texts, one must be able to locate relevant excerpts in lengthy texts, create a meaningful reading sequence for the passages, and establish crucial relations between different documents which may even be of various types (e.g., tables, graphs, pictures). However, empirical studies have shown that using complex or lengthy textual materials for learning purposes can be difficult, even for mature readers. For instance, high school and college students vary in their ability to build coherent reading sequences (Lodevijks, 1982; Wagner & Sternberg, 1987) and students apply more or less efficient strategies when searching textbook chapters to locate specific information (Dreher & Guthrie, 1990; Goldman & Saul, 1990).

Hypertext has been proposed as a means to support advanced learning activities that require sophisticated study strategies (Jacobson & Spiro, 1992; Spiro, Feltovitch, Jacobson, & Coulson, 1991). Two features of hypertext systems, in particular, may facilitate readers' access to textual information. First, hypertext systems offer various means to easily move through text units (embedded menus, search facilities, etc.). Second, in hypertext, textual information may be organized in a nonlinear way either through top-level structural units (i.e., tables of contents, indices) or through direct links between passages. According to Spiro et al. (1991), advanced learning in ill-structured domains requires crisscrossing, or the study of the same materials from different points of view. They propose that hypertext might promote a more thorough understanding of the conceptual organization of ill-structured domains as a result of these multiple connections between information units. So far, however, these contentions have received little empirical support (see the discussion by Dillon, in this volume).

In this chapter, we suggest that because of nonlinearity and easy movement, hypertext systems may provide an ideal environment for learning and reasoning about historical events and evidence. In fact, several hypertext development efforts have used history as an application domain and we start the first section by reviewing some of these early projects. Then we expand the motivation of applying hypertext systems to the problem of learning and reasoning in history by introducing the theoretical notion of an argument model as a method for representing the relation between different documents.

In the second part of the chapter, we describe a simple hypertext document presentation system that was developed primarily as a research tool. Then we report two studies on the use of hypertext presentation of multiple history documents by students at different levels of expertise. We focus on students' cognitive strategies, as evidenced by the records of their selections and study times in the hypertext system. We examine the influence of study-set composition and initial expertise on students' study strategies.

In the third part of the chapter, we report an empirical comparison of hypertext and linear document presentation formats. We studied how presentation format influences students' document selections and document learning. We discuss the implications of our findings for future hypertext research as well as for the design of educational hypertext.

USING HYPERTEXT TO SUPPORT
DOCUMENT-BASED LEARNING

Weyer's (1982) "dynamic book" was one of the earliest attempts to represent historical information through a hypertext-like system. The concept of a dynamic book maintained the linear nature of the written text, but provided the reader with a set of tools to facilitate the retrieval and selection of related information. The prototype used a high school history textbook and included two special navigation features; a hierarchical table of contents that enabled direct access to chapters, sections, and subsections, and a string-pattern matching facility to enable easy information search.

To test the efficacy of the system, Weyer had 16 high school students use the dynamic book to answer different types of questions. Weyer noted that the students had little difficulty using the simplest features of the system. However, the students had trouble using more advanced features such as the addition of items to a table of cross-references. Moreover, Weyer noted that searching the dynamic book to answer complex questions (e.g., questions that involved comparing information at various locations in the text) remained a complex cognitive task for high school students. In other words, although the dynamic book offered sophisticated search tools, it did not reduce the cognitive complexity of the task. Weyer concluded that novice users might need some training before they are able to use the advanced features of the dynamic book efficiently.

More recently, Shneiderman and his colleagues developed the HyperTIES system, a hypertext system that was used for several applications (Shneiderman, 1987), including a database on European history. They segmented the domain into a set of topics. Each topic was presented as a passage of text. Within each passage, several keywords were highlighted and could be selected, which led the reader to related topics in the database (see Koved & Shneiderman, 1986). A version of the database containing 106 articles was compared to its paper equivalent for question-answering tasks. The paper version resulted in faster search for simple fact retrieval questions. However, the users of the hypertext version performed equally rapidly for more complex items (Marchionini & Shneiderman, 1988; Shneiderman, 1989).

MuG (Eco, 1992) is another project for representing information about European culture and history using hypermedia technologies. The system includes three interconnected components; "Interactive Chronologies" of given periods where places and topics are connected to a thesaurus, a "Cardfile" containing reference cards and definitions, and a "Library" of hypermedia books about specific topics. The purpose of the MuG system is to serve as a "teaching aid" to university students. However, Eco (1992) did not mention any attempt to evaluate the system empirically.

A common principle guiding these endeavors is that hypertext presentation of multiple documents, with embedded links between related sources and search tools, will facilitate students' use of large amounts of textual information. These features may enhance the selection of relevant passages, the comparison of information, and the establishment of relationships between different types of information. However, several empirical studies have raised some doubt about the actual benefits of using hypertext compared to traditional presentation formats (e.g., print). The use of hypertext does not always foster better comprehension or learning (Rouet, 1992). In some studies, users actually found hypertext more difficult to read than linear text (Gordon, Gustavel, Moore, & Hankey, 1988; see also the review by Rouet and Levonen, in this volume).

A potential problem of evaluating many hypertext studies is that experimenters have tried to use hypertext to present in a nonlinear fashion texts that were primarily designed to be read in a fixed order. For instance, Gordon et al. (1988) used newspaper and journal articles as input materials for their study, and converted them into hypertext using informal subjective judgment. Converting linear text into hypertext may decrease comprehensibility of the materials, especially because coherence breaks down at the local and global levels (see Charney, in press; Foltz, 1992; Foltz, in this volume). Hypertext may be better adapted to the presentation of multiple text passages that did not originate from a single text. As Mynatt, Leventhal, Instone, Farhat, and Rohlman (1992) suggested, "hypertext . . . is perhaps a more natural medium for non-linear information with many interconnections. By non-linear information we mean information that can be understood in isolation, and that does not assume that previous (non-general) information has been acquired" (p. 20).

For problems that necessitate the use of vast amounts of information, readers may benefit from hypertext linking facilities. Hypertext may be used to connect related documents, and to facilitate cross-referencing between documents. However, there has been little empirical work on the use of hypertext as a multidocument environment for learning and reasoning.

A situation where intersource relationships are essential is the study of historical controversies. In a series of recent studies, we examined college students' ability to reason about the history of the Panama Canal, a theme that has had important consequences on the political relations between the United States and Central American countries throughout the 20th century (Britt, Rouet, Georgi, & Perfetti, 1994; Perfetti, Britt, & Georgi, 1995; Rouet, Britt, Mason, & Perfetti, 1996).

In their initial study, Perfetti et al. had 6 college students read four very long texts that offered various authors' perspectives on the events leading up to the building of a U.S.-controlled canal in Panama. Students were given the texts in a specific order. The subjects were also given treaties that the four authors used to support their positions. Perfetti et al. found that students were sensitive to several important features of these texts, for example, the fact that some authors were clearly biased in their interpretations. However, students easily changed their opinions after reading each text and did very little integration of information across texts. With one exception, they did not use the primary evidence (i.e., the critical treaties) that had been made available to them, and they did not feel that they needed other documents (although the second-hand accounts frequently referred to such documents). These students seemed to adopt a strategy of learning each individual text rather than constructing a single integrated representation of the events. Similarly, Wineburg (1991) found that high school students tended to rank a textbook excerpt as the most trustworthy type of document, and that they did not make use of written documents when evaluating the accuracy of paintings depicting the battle of Lexington. Thus, when using documents presented in traditional formats, students may rely on the simplest forms of discourse (e.g., an excerpt from a textbook) and ignore other forms of evidence.

This lack of integration on the students' part might be partially related to the cognitive load of using several sources of information. In fact, many researchers have recently demonstrated the potential cognitive cost of managing different sources of information (e.g., Reinking & Rickman, 1990; Sweller, Chandler, Tierney, & Cooper, 1990; Wright, 1991). The physical manipulation of several books or papers, added to the unfamiliarity of the discourse types found in certain documents (e.g., legal evidence), may render the task too complex for inexpert history students, who may rely on simpler strategies (e.g., get the basic story through the textbook). Computerized presentation of textual materials may benefit the reader by reducing the cost of manipulating and locating relevant pieces of information. A second reason students in the Perfetti et al. study may have failed to integrate the information across texts was because the texts were presented in a serial order, as four different "assignments."

We hypothesized that in order to enhance students' learning of the events and of the intersource relationships, we needed to present the students with a set of documents as a related whole with a more specific task such as solving a controversy. For instance, there is disagreement over whether or not U.S. military intervention in the 1903 Panamanian revolution was justified. There are many relevant documents available and some argue opposing points of view on this controversy. Other documents provide direct evidence for these arguments. Because these documents are interconnected, the reader is forced to create a representation of how the documents relate to each other. We refer to such a representation as a *global argument model* (Britt et al., 1994). This model is represented by a network of nodes and connecting links. Each node is a document and its source. Important source features, such as author and type of document, are included in the node. The links between the nodes depict the relationship between the documents. One example of a link is an "evidence" relation created by a specific citation of one document in another. A second type of link between two documents is an "opposed to" relation expressing that the two purport opposite points of view.

A student reading multiple documents covering a complex historical problem must identify the sources of information, how they contribute to the problem, and the relationships between sources. In other words, the student must build a representation of the global organization of the argument model. We suggest that hypertext may be used to facilitate cross-referencing between documents and may lead to more coherent global argument models built from several documents on the same topic.

In the next section, we present two studies that used a simple hypertext document presentation system. The primary purpose of these studies was to analyze U.S. college students' document learning strategies. In particular, we wanted to investigate their study strategies, and whether various factors (i.e., the composition of the study set and the students' evaluation of document usefulness) influenced their selection and reading patterns. The hypertext system was mainly used as an experimental device to allow the online study of students' reading strategies. Because the hypertext system was used as an experimental tool, we did not compare hypertext to print. And, the system was not designed to serve in real educational settings, but some of the results yield useful insights for the design of future applications.

STUDYING MULTIPLE DOCUMENTS IN A SIMPLE HYPERTEXT ENVIRONMENT: THE ROLE OF PRIMARY EVIDENCE AND DOMAIN EXPERTISE

An Experimental Document Presentation System

In our first two studies, we gave university students a set of seven documents on a controversy. They read the documents in a simplified hypertext environment that allowed the online presentation of the entire document set. The system was implemented using HyperCard on a Macintosh computer. The overall organization of this system is presented in Fig. 4.1.

Main Screen. The main screen presents general information about the controversy and the document set. On the left, a chronology window presents a list of basic facts that introduce the setting of the problem. On the upper right-hand side is the source selection area. This area presents a list of the available documents. Each document is represented in a clickable frame (or "button" in hypertext terminology). Only general information about the document is presented at this level; author, date, type of document. On the lower right-hand side is a task management area that contains buttons allowing the student to perform various tasks: Read the problem statement again (which appears as a pop-up field) or end the search.

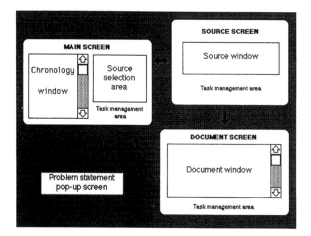

FIG. 4.1. Overview of the document presentation system.

Source Screen. Once a document button has been clicked, the extended source of the document is presented on the source screen. The extended source information includes author, date, title, type of document, and a short statement indicating the content of the document relative to the problem. The source screen also includes a task management area that allows the student to read the full document, read the problem statement again, or go back to the main screen.

Document Screen. If the student decides to read the document, then the text of the document is presented in a scrollable window on the document screen. The task management area allows the student to read the problem statement or to go back to the main screen. Moving back to the source screen is not possible; however, the document screen also contains the source information.

An example of a main screen is presented in Fig. 4.2. In this example, the system presents a set of documents about the U.S. intervention in the Panamanian revolution. The chronology window lists a series of main events with their dates and times. The source selection area lists the seven documents available; two excerpts from historians' books ("Norman" and "Wilson"[1]); two speeches by participants (Carmack and Roosevelt), an excerpt from a history textbook, and two pieces of primary evidence (military correspondence and U.S.–Colombia Treaty). In order to keep the system simple to use, we did not include any direct link between documents in this version. Such a system with direct links is presented later on in this chapter.

A noticeable feature of this system is that it mixes linear and nonlinear presentation formats. At the level of each text or document, the text is presented in its original linear format whereas at the global level of a study set, movement

---

[1]Except for participants, authors' names are fictitious.

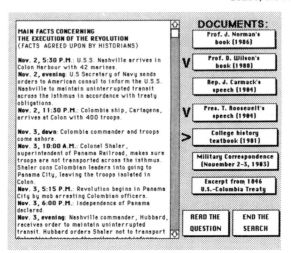

FIG. 4.2.   Example of main screen in the document presentation system. (A "V" sign next to a source in the selection area indicates that the source has been previously selected. The ">" sign indicates the last selected source.)

between documents is nonlinear. The global level (main screen) allows for transitions among the different local level texts (source and document screens). An obvious advantage of such a presentation mode is that it decreases the burden associated with the physical manipulation of documents. The documents are made available instantly through a simple clickable list of items.

It has been established that even simple hypertexts can be confusing for inexperienced users (Charney, in press; Rouet, 1992). Consequently, the usability of our document presentation system was assessed by running a pilot experiment. Five graduate students and faculty members of the University of Pittsburgh were asked to study two document sets using the system. The subjects were asked to report any difficulty or suggestion about the system or the task. All the subjects managed to select and read the documents, and no major difficulty was reported. However, minor aspects of the hypertext interface (e.g., location and naming of buttons) were improved following subjects' reports. The pilot experiment was also useful in calibrating the materials and the procedure (allowed study time, directions, etc.).

The Effect of Document Type on Study Strategies

The primary purpose of Experiment 1 (Rouet et al., 1996) was to find out how students would use different types of documents when learning about a history problem. More specifically, we wanted to determine whether letting students read primary documents (e.g., treaties, correspondence) would improve their representation of the controversy, an issue that has received conflicting evidence in past studies. Another objective was to find out whether the composition of the study set had any impact on students' selection strategies in the hypertext.

We used four controversies related to the history of the Panama Canal (e.g., "Was the U.S. military intervention in the 1903 Panamanian revolution justified?"). For each controversy, we prepared a chronological list of the main facts, and a study set made of seven documents; two secondary documents (historical essays arguing opposite interpretations), two intermediate documents (accounts written by participants arguing opposite sides), a Textbook-like excerpt (a neutral descriptive account written by the experimenters), and two primary documents (treaties or correspondence).

Each document set (or each controversy) can be represented on a global level as a series of nodes (i.e., individual documents) connected by their relations to each other. Fig. 4.3 shows an example of the global level for controversy 2. Each document node includes the position the document takes. In Fig. 4.3, the neutrality–bias dimension is indicated by columns. The most unbiased documents are in the center column and the more opinionated documents are in the right and left columns. Relationships between documents are shown as arrows in Fig. 4.3. An "evidence" relation is the arrow between the 1846 U.S.–Colombia treaty and President Roosevelt's 1904 speech. President Roosevelt directly cited this treaty in his speech. A second example of an evidence link is the arrow between the 1846 U.S.–Colombia treaty and Professor Norman's historical essay. In his essay, he used the treaty to support his claim that U.S. intervention in Panama was not justified.

As illustrated in Fig. 4.3, primary documents are central in studying the issue because they are cited in almost all the other documents. To create a control

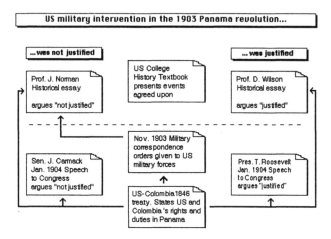

FIG. 4.3. Global argument structure for the problem "Was the U.S. military intervention in the Panamanian revolution justified?" (after Britt, Rouet, Georgi, & Perfetti, 1994).

condition, we selected two additional secondary documents for each controversy. These additional secondary documents replaced the primary documents. Half the subjects received a study set containing the primary documents ("primary group"), and the other half received a study set containing the additional secondary documents ("secondary group"). Comparing students' behavior in the primary and secondary conditions allowed us to study the effects of primary information availability.

The subjects were 24 college students with varying experience in history. However, none of the students was a history major. In the first session, students were tested for their history and geography knowledge and then given a background text. Subject assignment to the primary group or to the secondary group was balanced for gender, history, knowledge, and reading ability.

In a second session, the students were trained on the hypertext system using a sample set of documents. Then the students were asked to study the four controversies. For each controversy, the students were given a maximum of fifteen minutes to study the document set. At the end of the study period, the students were asked to write an essay expressing their opinion about the controversy and to evaluate the documents' usefulness and trustworthiness.

Variability of Students' Selection Strategies

All subjects were given a menu listing the available documents in the following order; two secondary, two intermediate, one textbook, and either two primary (primary group) or two additional secondary (secondary group). Subjects were allowed to read the sources and documents in any order and as many times as they wanted, within the 15-minute period. We analyzed students' selection strategies and found that they were highly variable across students and problems. In fact, only one subject selected the documents in an identical order for all four problems. However, there were some notable patterns relating to the initial document reading order and reviewing behavior that we discuss later. To illustrate the different patterns, we have included four typical selection sequences in Fig. 4.4.

Initial Reading Order. Both subjects A and B read the documents in the list order, that is, the order the documents were mentioned in the menu. They selected and read secondary document #1 first, followed by secondary document #2, continuing in this order until they had read each document once. In contrast, subjects C and D read the documents in an idiosyncratic order, or an order different from the list order. Subject C read an intermediate document first, then the textbook, then the two pieces of primary evidence. Finally, the subject read intermediate document 1 and the two historical essays. Subject D read each of the documents in the reverse order listed in the menu.

In selecting the initial reading order of the documents, there was a general preference for subjects to take into account source information and the specific

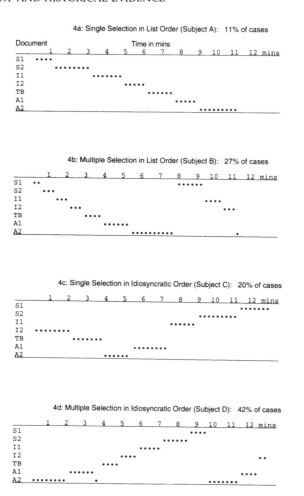

FIG. 4.4. Types of selection sequences in the document presentation system. The documents are listed on the left in their screen presentation order; S1, S2 = secondary documents; I1, I2 = intermediate documents; TB = textbook; A1, A2 = additional documents (i.e., primary documents for the primary group, secondary documents for the secondary group).

controversy statement. Most of the selections (62%) were in an idiosyncratic order and most of the subjects (79%) selected the documents in a unique order for at least one of the four controversies. On the other hand, strict list order selections represented 38% of the sequences, and 21% of the subjects never initially read the documents out of the given order. Thus, although they were instructed to select the documents "wisely" because of the time constraints, many subjects still tended to follow the proposed order of presentation. Most of these list order selections were due to 7 subjects who consistently (i.e., on three or four of the controversies) used this selection strategy, all but one of which were in the primary group.

There was a clear influence of document set on the tendency for subjects to deviate from the list order. In the primary group, half of the subjects consistently read the documents in the list order, whereas the other half of the subjects consistently read the documents in an idiosyncratic order. Subjects in the secondary group were, in general, more daring. Only 8% of the subjects consistently read the documents in the list order, whereas 75% of the subjects consistently read the documents in an idiosyncratic order. The remaining 17% varied between selecting their own order and selecting based on the list order.

This preference for subjects in the primary group to read the documents in the list order may be a result of the logical order of presentation (secondary [S1 and S2], intermediate [I1 and I2], textbook [TB], and primary documents [A1 and A2]) or because all the documents were very useful, making discriminability based on source information alone difficult. The secondary group, in contrast, had four documents of the same type (i.e., S1, S2, A1, and A2 were all secondary documents). In this case, the textbook and the intermediate documents may have appeared more salient.

When documents were selected in an idiosyncratic order, the documents available influenced the initial documents selected. On 54% of the occasions, the first documents that primary subjects selected were the primary and intermediate documents or the primary documents and the textbook. In contrast, the subjects in the secondary group almost never (3%) initially selected the matching documents (additional-secondary and intermediate documents or the additional-secondary documents and the textbook). The secondary subjects tended instead to select intermediate documents and the textbook first (64% of occasions). The primary subjects rarely selected this combination first (4%). Thus, the composition of the study set had an important influence on students' selection strategies.

This result is consistent with the way subjects evaluated the documents after the study task. Subjects in the primary group preferred the primary documents and the textbook, selecting to read them first and later ranking them most trustworthy and useful. Subjects in the secondary group preferred the textbook and intermediate documents. This suggests that subjects tend to select first what seems important to them.

Reviewing Behavior.   On only a minority (31%) of the occasions did the subjects choose not to review at least one document. Subjects A and C in Fig. 4.4 illustrate two different patterns of nonreviewers. On a majority (69%) of the occasions, subjects chose to review at least one document. Subjects B and D in Fig. 4.4 illustrate two different patterns of reviewers. Subject B started by selecting and reading all the documents in their presentation order, in a way similar to subject A. However, subject B then reviewed four of the documents; one of the historical essays, the two intermediate documents, and (briefly) one of the primary documents. Subject D selected the documents in an order different from the list order and reviewed several of them; the two primary documents and the second intermediate document.

Unlike the order of selection, there was no influence of document type on whether a subject reviewed or not. Ten subjects were consistent reviewers and 10 subjects were consistent nonreviewers. This was equal for both conditions.

Domain Expertise and Document Study

In a second experiment, we used similar materials and procedures to examine novice and expert history students' use of document information (Rouet, Favart, Britt, & Perfetti, 1995). Materials from Controversies 2 and 4 were translated into French. Eleven French psychology graduate students and 8 French history graduate students were trained on the hypertext and asked to study the two controversies. All the subjects received document sets including primary documents.

Again, the selection strategies varied widely across subjects. Only 2 subjects (one novice, one expert) selected the documents in the list order. They did so for both problems. All the other subjects (89%) selected the documents in different orders.

Although the selection order varied across subjects, we were able to identify a few regularities. For instance, subjects in both groups tended to select the textbook early in the sequence: About 50% of the subjects (6 novices and 4 experts) selected the textbook as the first, second, or third document in both problems. An additional 25% (4 novices and 1 expert) did so for one of the two controversies.

For Problem 2, the primary documents tended to be selected early in the study period (like subject D in Fig. 4.4). In fact, in Problem 2, 68% of the subjects selected both primary documents among the first three documents. This result may reflect the fact that Problem 2 ("was the Hay–Bunau–Varilla Treaty a good deal for Panama?") more directly focused on the primary documents. However, other explanations (e.g., familiarity with the task or the document set) may be considered.

Thus, although study sequences were variable, the textbook was generally read early, and the same was true for primary documents in Problem 2. As in the first experiment, those documents were ranked among the most useful and trustworthy. We did not find any systematic difference between novice and expert history students in the selection, review, or reading time of the documents.

Synthesis and Discussion

Previous studies on multiple text reading have shown that students vary in their ability to construct meaningful arrangements from a set of information units (e.g., Lodevijks, 1982). The diversity of the study sequences collected in the two studies summarized in this section indicates that students also vary in the way they handle a multiple-document study task.

Some students tended to follow passively the order of presentation, although in both studies they were instructed to select the documents wisely to cope with the time limit. However, in both studies a majority of students organized their selections in a more personal way and the selection patterns of these students were influenced by the composition of the study set. This indicates that the source information given in the main screen selection area was actually used by the students. Students were able to prioritize the documents' importance, and they tended to first study those documents that they judged most important. In both studies, the textbook excerpt and primary documents were considered important both in terms of subjective ranking and in terms of selection sequences.

In sum, even inexpert history students possess some prototypical knowledge about document types (e.g., textbook, primary sources) that they use to find their way in the document presentation system. This finding is consistent with previous studies on expert reading strategies (Dillon, 1991). However, the number and diversity of text types used in our studies increased the amount of relevant knowledge, which may explain in part the diversity of study strategies. An issue that is left unanswered is whether some of these strategies lead to better learning.

Experts and novices did not differ significantly in their study strategies, due in part to the large within-group diversity of selection patterns. However, the specificity of our study conditions must be recalled here: In both studies, students were made clearly aware of the type of problems they were studying. Furthermore, the system was designed to force students to consider source information when studying the materials. These rather specific study conditions may have influenced students' selection patterns. It is possible that different conditions (a more ill-defined problem situation, a less structured information environment—say, a library instead of our document presentation system) would elicit novice–expert differences.

Finally, in both studies there were differences across problems. The nature of the problem seemed to influence students' selection strategies. This indicates that their strategy is not planned independently from the problem. Rather, the way students handle their navigation in a set of documents also depends on the nature of the problem.

THE INFLUENCE OF LINEAR VERSUS HYPERTEXT PRESENTATION FORMAT ON STUDENTS' MULTIPLE-DOCUMENT STUDY STRATEGIES

The Effect of Presentation Format on Reading Text and Hypertext

Our studies using the simple document presentation system demonstrated that such a system allows effective study and information acquisition even for students with minimal experience with hypertext. This finding may be considered rather positive given the numerous usability problems noted in the hypertext literature (e.g., Rouet, 1992). However, our studies did not allow us to evaluate whether the hypertext format had any effect on how students learn from documents, or even on how they organize their study of the documents.

Previous studies comparing hypertext and linear presentations of the same materials have had mixed results. In a study by Gordon et al. (1988), the linear presentation format (i.e., passages presented in a fixed order) resulted in better comprehension of central ideas compared to hierarchical hypertext presentation. Furthermore, under "casual reading" directions, subjects recalled more central information with linear presentation, and found the hypertext format more effortful. Especially informative was hypertext readers' feeling that they "didn't know what was behind the door," that is, they were not sure what information they would find after clicking on an item.

On the other hand, a study by Dee-Lucas and Larkin (1992) found some positive outcomes of a structured hypertext format. Dee-Lucas and Larkin compared three presentation formats of the same 9-unit expository text on electricity; linear, hypertext with alphabetic index, and hypertext with hierarchical index. When subjects were given a general comprehension task, the two hypertext formats resulted in a larger breadth of recall (subjects recalled information from more units). Furthermore, the hierarchical hypertext allowed faster selection and resulted in better memory for item location in the Table of Contents. However, in a second experiment where subjects were given a summary task, the between-format differences were nonsignificant. Dee-Lucas and Larkin concluded that specific reading directions may override the effects of different presentation formats (see also Dee-Lucas, in this volume).

Given the inconclusive evidence, we have started to compare several presentation formats with respect to their consequences on study strategies and learning. In Experiment 3, we examined whether a structured hypertext can lead to students building a better representation of the relationship between multiple documents in a historical problem.

When reading several documents that relate to a common problem, a student must form an argument model or a representation of the hierarchical organization of the document set (Britt et al., 1994). If students access one document using a hypertext link because they read a citation of that document in a second source, then they should have an enhanced connection between those two documents. In this case the connection should be functional. These strong, meaningful connections should yield better global argument models.

Method

To test the effectiveness of hypertext in helping a student build an argument model, we prepared two sets of nine documents about two aspects of the history of the Panama Canal: the Panamanian revolution and the Hay–Bunau–Varilla Treaty. The table of contents for controversy one is shown in Fig. 4.5. Each

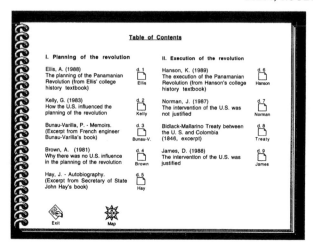

FIG. 4.5.   Table of contents for the linear format. Documents can be located using page numbers and the "next page" button.

problem was comprised of two aspects or subcontroversies, each of which had a textbook passage that presented factual accounts of that subproblem. For instance, in Problem 1, one textbook passage presented the "planning of the revolution" subproblem and the other textbook passage presented the "execution of the revolution" subproblem. There were four historians' accounts presenting conflicting interpretations of the subproblems. For instance, Professor Kelly argued that the United States helped plan the revolt in Panama whereas Professor Brown claimed the opposite. The historians' arguments were based on several types of available evidence. For each problem, there were three primary documents that contained evidence used in the historians' accounts. For instance, revolutionary leader Bunau-Varilla's memoirs mentioned a meeting with President Roosevelt. This document supported the "United States helped" interpretation.

Thus, for each problem, the documents could be organized hierarchically as the map in Fig. 4.6 depicts. Each textbook passage mentioned two opposite interpretations and each interpretation was based on one primary document. For one subproblem, the arguments were based on unique primary documents whereas for the other subproblem, the arguments were based on a common primary document.

The document sets were presented online using either a linear or a hypertext navigation format. In the linear format, the system included a table of contents, the nine documents, and a "map" showing the hierarchical organization of the documents, each on a separate page. The subjects could go from one page to another by pushing "next page" and "previous page" buttons. In addition, the subjects could access directly the first page (table of contents) and the last page (map) from any other page of the system. The table of contents page of the linear format is shown in Fig. 4.5 and the map page is shown in Fig. 4.6.

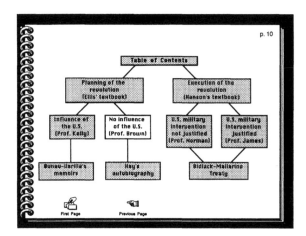

FIG. 4.6. Dynamic hierarchical map for the hypertext format. Document from which map was called up is highlighted.

In the hypertext format, the system included the same 11 pages from the linear format; a table of contents, nine documents, and a hierarchical map. However, the tools for navigating the system were quite different. First, there was no "next page" button on the table of contents page. Instead, the icon next to each document was directly clickable, allowing direct access to the documents. Second, each document page included buttons that allowed the reader to go directly to referred-to documents. An example of a document page in the hypertext format is presented in Fig. 4.7.

The document presented in Fig. 4.7 contained a reference to another document, Secretary of State John Hay's autobiography. The "Hay" icon in the lower right corner of Fig. 4.7 represented this embedded reference. The "Hay" icon could be clicked on and the excerpt from Hay's book appeared. In addition, each document page contained a backtracking icon representing the document previously read. In the example of Fig. 4.7, the subject selected Brown's text after reading the textbook. Clicking on the "textbook" icon allowed the subject to go to the textbook. The backtracking icon was dynamically modified as a function of subjects' navigation in the system.

Both the hypertext and the linear formats contained a map showing the hierarchical organization of the documents. The map page was very similar across formats, except for the navigation technique. In the linear system the map was represented as the last page. The map could be accessed either by flipping through the document pages or by clicking the "last page" icon. From the map page, students could either flip back through the document pages or go back directly to the table of contents. In the hypertext format the map could be directly called up from any page. The page from which the map had been called up was highlighted (see Fig. 4.6). Clicking on the map resulted in the previous page

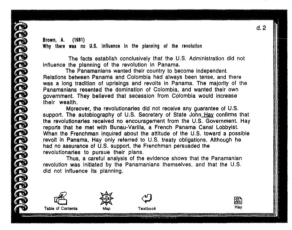

FIG. 4.7.   An example document in the hypertext format. "Hay" button allows direct access to the Hay Document. The "textbook" button allows backtracking to previous document.

being displayed again. Thus, in the hypertext format the map was a "pop up" type of page.

In addition to the format, we also manipulated the organization of the document set. In the structured condition (shown in Figs. 4.5 and 4.6), the documents were organized in a manner that corresponded to the hierarchical structure, with Subproblem 1 (on the left of Fig. 4.5) beginning with the textbook, followed by a secondary document, followed by the cited primary document, and so forth. In the scrambled condition, the documents were organized in a random order that conveyed no information about how the documents related to each other in a hierarchical structure.

The one within-subject factor was argument support in secondary documents. Each secondary document included two main arguments supporting the author's claim. One argument was supported by available evidence whereas the other was either supported by unavailable evidence or not supported at all. For example, the author in Fig. 4.7 claimed that the United States did not influence the planning of the revolution. To support this claim, he provided two arguments: The Pana-manians always wanted their freedom (A1), and the revolutionaries did not receive any guarantee of U.S. support (A2). No evidence was brought in support of A1; A2 had an explicit reference to a document that provided evidence (i.e., Hay's autobiography). The purpose of this factor was to find out whether explicit support would increase subjects' memory for the arguments.

Table 4.1 provides an outline of the factors manipulated in this study.

The subjects were 44 college students with various experience in history. However, none of the students was a history major. In session one, subjects were first tested on their history and geography knowledge, and then given a back-ground text to read. Then the students were trained on the hypertext system using

TABLE 4.1
Experimental Manipulations in Study 3

Factors	Levels	Definition
Between subject factors		
Presentation format	Linear	Documents linked in linear fashion. Forward and backward page turning.
	Hypertext	Documents linked hierarchically. Direct menu selection and embedded reference links.
Top-level organization	Structured	Documents listed in logical order.
	Scrambled	Documents listed in scrambled order.
Within subject factors		
Argument support	Supported	Argument supported by available documentary evidence.
	Unsupported	Argument not supported by available evidence.

a sample set of documents about a different topic. The experimenter trained the subjects by modeling the study strategy the subjects were to use for all problems. In the hypertext condition, they were asked to read the document by following the links. After they had read each document once, they could review the documents in any order. In the linear condition, they were asked to read the documents by paging forward, reading one document at a time in a linear order. After they had read each document once, they could review the documents in any order. The subjects were then given all posttests described later. Prior to the second session, subjects were assigned to one of the four conditions to make the groups approximately balanced for gender, history knowledge, and reading ability. Twelve subjects were assigned to the structured hypertext condition, 12 to the structured linear condition, 10 to the scrambled hypertext condition, and 10 to the scrambled linear condition.

In a second session, the experimenter again modeled the study strategy and reminded the subjects to read the documents in the specified order. The subjects were given 20 minutes to study the document set. After the study period, they answered comprehension questions, completed an author recognition task, and recalled the authors' arguments and evidence given to support the authors' claims.

In the third session, subjects followed the same procedure used in Session 2 for the second controversy except after completing all the posttests, they were given a blank map of the document set and asked to fill it in with author names and titles. Then they were given a sheet with the nine documents in random order and asked to recall the page numbers of the nine documents.

We hypothesized that the hypertext presentation format would facilitate students' learning. One advantage of hypertext over linear print presentation format is that the argument model is functional. The reader can use this discourse structure to access the documents by clicking on icons located next to the source. The relations between documents (both the source and content, and the claim and evidence) should be more salient in the hypertext environment. Thus, structured hypertext presentation may help subjects build an argument model and hence, facilitate the understanding of the controversy. In the hypertext condition, the embedded icons and the backtracking icon allowed students to go back and forth between related documents. We hypothesized that this could strengthen the relation between arguments and evidence, thus facilitating the representation of the argument model.

During the debriefing, we were able to ask approximately half the subjects whether they liked the presentation system and whether they felt lost at any point. None of our subjects in any of the four conditions reported difficulties with the system and no subjects felt lost. Thus, even the subjects in the scrambled condition did not report problems.

Analysis of Subjects' Study Sequences

Study sequences (i.e., the order in which the subjects selected and read the documents during the 20 minute study period) were highly variable across presentation conditions. Figure 4.8 gives an example of a subject's study sequence for Problem 1 in each of the four conditions. The examples presented in Fig. 4.8 were chosen because they exhibit features typical of what was observed in the group. In Fig. 4.8, each page of the system is represented as a line. The sequence is represented chronologically, from left to right. A "•" indicates that the subject stopped on a page for 3 seconds or more (long selection). An "o" indicates that the subject stopped on the page for less than three seconds (short selection).

The subject in Fig. 4.8a went through the whole series of documents from the first to the last page twice. Then she went through the list one more time backward, skipping some of the documents (I1, S2, P1). In the structured linear condition, 92% of the subjects went through the whole list at least twice during their study period.

The study sequence in Fig. 4.8b (structured hypertext) can be subdivided into two phases: In the first phase (Selections 1–24) the subject used mostly direct links between the documents. The subject went back to the table of contents only once during the study of each subproblem (Steps 9 and 15). In the second phase (Steps 25–39), the subject used the table of contents icons to access and review some of the documents. About 60% of the structured hypertext subjects used direct links at the beginning of their study period and then shifted to the table of contents.

The subject in Fig. 4.8c (scrambled linear) did not go through the list of documents in their presentation order. Instead, she decided in advance what document to read, and then skipped as many documents as necessary to access the target document. This allowed the subject to study each subproblem one after the other; Subproblem 1 (Selections 1–28), Subproblem 2 (Selections 29–53), and Subproblem 1 again (Selections 54–67). Eighty-five percent of subjects in the scrambled linear condition organized their study period as a function of

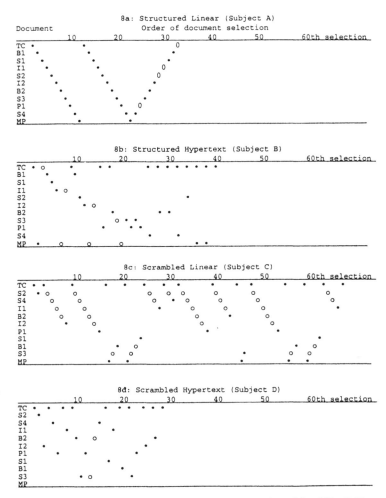

FIG. 4.8. Sample study sequences from each experimental condition (TC = Table of Contents, S1–S4 = Secondary documents, B1–B2 = Textbook passages, I1–I2 = intermediate documents, P1 = primary document).

subproblem structure, studying each subproblem separately at least once. Notice that this strategy resulted in a lot of page turning. However, the subject in Fig. 4.8c tried to overcome this burden by using either the table of contents or the map as a starting point depending on which was closest to the target document.

Finally the subject in Fig. 4.8d, although in a hypertext condition, did not make much use of the direct links between documents. Instead, he used the table of contents for half of his selections. Like the subject in Fig. 4.8d, 55% of the scrambled hypertext subjects used the table of contents for half or more of their selections.

Based on these preliminary observations, we studied three main parameters of the subjects' study sequences; total number of text selections, number of long selections (i.e., 3 seconds or more) and proportion of selections made using the table of contents (as opposed to direct links or page turning). Table 4.2 shows the value of these parameters as a function of problem, presentation format, and organization. Results were analyzed using a three way mixed-design analysis of variance with format and organization as between factors and problem as a within factor.

There was a significant Format × Organization interaction on the total number of text selections, $F(1, 40) = 21.36$, $p < .001$. The number of selections was much larger in the scrambled linear format than in the other three formats (Table 4.2). This larger number of text selections was due to the fact that subjects had to flip through pages in order to locate documents of interest. Indeed, when only the number of long text selections was considered, there was no significant

TABLE 4.2
Parameters of Subjects' Study Sequences

	Problem number		
Group	P1		P2
Total number of text selections			
Structured			
Linear	32.2 (11.2)		29.6 (8.0)
Hypertext	28.4 (10.1)		24.4 (9.4)
Scrambled			
Linear	56.3 (20.6)		55.6 (17.9)
Hypertext	18.4 (6.1)		21.7 (9.3)
Number of selections longer than 3 sec.			
Structured			
Linear	23.7 (6.9)		21.4 (6.9)
Hypertext	24.6 (8.7)		21.0 (7.9)
Scrambled			
Linear	21.3 (9.2)		24.0 (11.4)
Hypertext	17.3 (5.6)		18.6 (6.1)
Percent of selections using table of contents			
Structured			
Linear	8.54 (3.20)		7.99 (2.86)
Hypertext	25.32 (11.38)		38.91 (17.73)
Scrambled			
Linear	19.49 (9.46)		16.14 (9.37)
Hypertext	50.36 (20.27)		49.49 (21.77)

Note. Standard deviation is given in parentheses.

difference across presentation conditions (Table 4.2). These analyses confirm that in the scrambled linear format, subjects did not follow passively the random ordering of the documents. Instead, they tried to build coherent study sequences.

The table of contents was used significantly more to choose documents both in the hypertext, $F(1, 40) = 52.46$, $p < .001$, and in the scrambled conditions, $F(1, 40) = 12.68$, $p < .001$ (Table 4.2). In addition, there was a significant interaction between format, structure, and problem, $F(1, 40) = 4.31$, $p < .05$. This interaction reflected an increase in the use of the table of contents from Problem 1 to Problem 2, but only in the structured hypertext condition. Thus, structured hypertext subjects tended to give up the modeled direct link strategy in Problem 2, and to use the table of contents instead. The scrambled hypertext subjects used the table of contents much more often in both Problem 1 and Problem 2.

Subjects in the linear conditions did not use the table of contents as much. However, they did so more often when the documents were presented in a scrambled order, suggesting that subjects needed to study the top level structure more thoroughly when its organization was less obvious.

Apart from the increase in table of contents usage in the structured hypertext group, the results were very similar across problems, which suggests that the effects of presentation format on subjects' study strategies were to a large extent independent from the problem as well as from the degree of familiarity with the task.

Memory for the Structure of the Document Set

We gave subjects two surprise tasks after the final problem. The first task, map completion, assessed implicit learning of the hierarchical structure of the document set. Subjects were given a blank map of the organization of the nine documents (a filled in map is shown in Fig. 4.6). They were asked to fill in each box with the source information that had been previously shown on the map, the document title and the author's name. It was expected that due to the embedded evidence links available to the hypertext subjects, they should have a better argument model or representation of the hierarchical structure of the set. The mean number of correct map items (titles and author names) is presented in Table 4.3. The only significant difference was that the subjects given scrambled documents recalled fewer items than the subjects given structured documents, $F(1, 39) = 26.63$, $p < .01$, (3.95 vs. 10.5). There was no map recall advantage for hypertext subjects compared to linear subjects. In fact, there was a nonsignificant trend for the linear subjects in the structured condition to recall more items. This suggests that hypertext subjects did not build a more coherent argument model.

One possible explanation is that the structured hypertext subjects were less likely to follow the links in Problem 2 and did not study the map as much as the linear subjects. In fact, we found a significant difference in map study time between the structured hypertext condition and the other three conditions. Subjects in the

TABLE 4.3
Mean Map Items (of a Possible 18) and Page Numbers (of a Possible 9)
Correctly Recalled in the Four Conditions

	Variable	
Group	Map	Page Numbers
Structured		
Linear	11.9	6.0
Hypertext	9.1	4.6
Scrambled		
Linear	3.6	4.1
Hypertext	4.3	0.9

structured linear condition spent an average of 74 seconds on the map compared to 29 seconds in the structured hypertext condition, 17 seconds in the scrambled linear condition, and 22 seconds in the scrambled hypertext condition.

In addition, because the map completion task was not under time pressure, some subjects stated that they were able to use their knowledge of the linear ordering to reconstruct the documents in the map task. Longer map study time and map reconstruction may partially explain why there was no advantage of hypertext format on the map task.

The second surprise task we gave subjects after the last problem was the page number task which was derived to assess implicit learning of the linear organization of the document set. Subjects were given a random list of the nine documents and they were asked to fill in the page number or document number for each. It was expected that because the linear subjects were restricted to forward and backward selections, they would have a better representation of the linear ordering of the document set. The mean number of correct page numbers is presented in Table 4.3. First, as in the map task, subjects given scrambled documents recalled significantly fewer correct page numbers than subjects given structured documents, $F(1, 39) = 12.18$, $p < .01$ (2.25 vs. 5.3). There was also an advantage for linear subjects to recall more than hypertext subjects, regardless of structure, $F(1, 39) = 8.33$, $p < .01$. This suggests that linear subjects did form a better linear representation of the document set.

Memory for Arguments

One of the posttests we gave subjects following each problem was the argument recall task. We provided subjects with the source and claim of each of the secondary documents and they were to recall the arguments and evidence that the author gave to support the claim. Table 4.4 gives the mean number of arguments recalled. Collapsing the two problems, we found a main effect for document structure, $F(1, 39) = 8.55$, $p < .01$, and a marginal effect of the format of pres-

TABLE 4.4
Mean Number of Arguments and Evidence Correctly Recalled
in the Four Conditions

Group	Argument Recall
Structured	
Linear	23.7
Hypertext	25.3
Scrambled	
Linear	23.8
Hypertext	15.8

entation, $F(1, 39) = 4.1, p < .05$. However, as Table 4.4 shows, these main effects are really due to a significant interaction between document structure and format of presentation, $F(1, 39) = 9.0$, $p < .01$. Presentation format did not lead to differential recall of the arguments and evidence when the documents where presented in a structured order, but linear presentation did lead to better recall when the documents were scrambled. Therefore, when subjects are given a document set that is structured to reflect a meaningful organization of the documents, hypertext links are not detrimental to student learning. However, we expected hypertext links to enhance argument recall and this did not occur. If, on the other hand, the documents are given to the subjects in a scrambled order, with no top-down information about how the documents are structured, then there will be a disadvantage to hypertext presentation format. This result is consistent with the Dee-Lucas and Larkin (1992) findings.

Discussion

The two presentation variables (structured vs. scrambled and linear vs. hypertext) influenced subjects' navigation in the document set during the study period. In the scrambled conditions, subjects did not fully comply with the modeled navigation pattern. Scrambled linear subjects tended to reconstruct a meaningful study sequence out of the scrambled order of presentation. Scrambled hypertext subjects tended to use the table of contents instead of the direct links. Moreover, structured hypertext subjects tended to depart from the modeled pattern in Problem 2. They used the table of contents more often, in a way similar to subjects using the scrambled hypertext.

Preference for overview structure over direct links is compatible with the results of previous studies (McKnight, Dillon, & Richardson, 1990). Our expectation that direct links would be more usable in our system because they were unambiguous was not confirmed. A possible explanation is that the two sets of links (table of contents, direct links) resulted in conflicting cognitive representations of the document set organization (e.g., a survey type vs. a route type of representation). Edwards and Hardman (1989) found evidence that a mixed linking structure (e.g., a hierarchy plus an index) was more difficult to use than a system providing just one type of link (see also Tripp & Robby, 1990).

In any case, our results clearly indicate that even inexperienced subjects can compensate for a nonideal presentation format by choosing documents in a meaningful order. Except in the structured linear condition, the subjects tended to depart from the modeled strategy. The alternate strategies they used tended to reconstruct global coherence and to use the table of contents more often. Two tentative interpretations may be suggested: Either the modeled strategies were cognitively inadequate, or they were adequate but inapplicable given time constraints. Following the latter interpretation, subjects might have planned their activity in an opportunistic fashion, a feature reported in other complex cognitive task domains (e.g., Guindon, 1990).

Our expectation that structured hypertext presentation would improve subjects' representation of the argument model was not supported. Overall, we found that subjects performed equally well in the structured hypertext and linear conditions. The only effect of presentation format was actually a deficit in the scrambled hypertext condition. These findings confirm the strong need for top-level structure when dealing with complex information systems (see also Foltz, in this volume).

Several reasons may explain why the structured hypertext condition failed to result in better learning. First, subjects received much background information prior to their use of the document set. The knowledge acquired before studying the documents might have reduced the effect of representing reference relations. Second, the structured index and map (which linear subjects spent more time studying) may have sufficed to allow linear subjects to build a representation of the relationships between sources.

Other possible reasons for the lack of influence of presentation format in the structured condition may have to do with task definition. The task of understanding the controversy was a rather specific one, and may have offset the influence of format (Dee-Lucas & Larkin, 1992). Moreover, memory for content was not specifically meausured by any of our posttests. For instance, we did not use any "breadth of recall" test. Thus, our experiment did not resolve the issue of how presentation format affects learning from multiple documents. Experiments involving other types of tasks (e.g., information search or general learning) and posttests (e.g., comprehension and memory tests) may still reveal an effect of hypertext versus linear presentation format.

GENERAL DISCUSSION AND CONCLUSION

In this chapter, we reported a series of studies in which we explored the potential of hypertext for document-based history learning. So far, most hypertext studies have used hypertext to present initially linear texts in nonlinear formats. In contrast, we used hypertext to present multiple documents according to simple hierarchical formats. Our approach aimed at avoiding the disruptive effects of transforming linear text into text networks (Gordon et al., 1988; Foltz, in this volume). Rather, we used hypertext presentation as a means to decrease the burden of manipulating multiple printed documents.

We used the hypertext linking facilities to represent between-document relationships. More specifically, we used hypertext to represent the argument model, that is, the global relationships (rhetorical, expository, and argumentative) among a set documents (Britt et al., 1994).

In the first series of studies, both novice and expert history students generally reported favorable impressions after using the document presentation systems. The simple hierarchical representation did not seem to cause any orientation problem, and subjects never requested external help after the training period.

The study of subjects' selection sequences revealed a diversity of study strategies. The strategies reflected subjects' independence or initiative toward the proposed organization of the materials. A first and rather passive strategy consisted in simply reading the series of documents as they were presented on the main screen list. This strategy was observed in 39% of the cases with U.S. college students and in 11% of the cases with French graduate students. Given that the main difference between the two populations was academic level, we suggest that general literacy results in students being more active toward the proposed structure of the information. By more active we mean that students build up personalized sequences of document reading, selecting first the documents that seem most important to them. This emphasizes the need to consider "environmental affordances" when studying the cognitive processes at work in complex information processing tasks (Wright, 1993).

In the second study, we compared linear and hypertext presentation formats of the same set of documents. We did not find any evidence for the advantage of one of the presentation formats over the other as far as document learning is concerned. However, we did find that representation of top-level organization of the document set is a crucial factor of usability and effectiveness. We also found some influence of document availability on students' memory for arguments. This argues in favor of letting students study directly from primary materials at all levels of history instruction.

Finally, our studies allow a few reflections on the design of educational hypertext systems. For instance, it is important for students to keep track of their study objectives when dealing with large amounts of information. In our first study, a "read the question" button allowed students to review the problem statement. In both experiments, this option was used by a majority of students. We suggest that when no explicit question or problem statement is available, hypertext systems include some note-taking facility so as to let the students make explicit their objectives and possibly review them as their study of the documents progresses. Also, students' previous document selection should be marked to alleviate the burden of remembering past selections (see Rouet, 1990).

Another important aspect of multidocument hypertext systems is the identification of nodes and links. In our approach, this was made simple by the homogeneous status of the hypertext nodes: All the nodes are document excerpts. Also, the linking between documents was kept very simple: In the second study, all the links corresponded to reference relationships. Thus, students were able to base their navigation decisions on unambiguous knowledge of the destination of buttons (thus avoiding the "what's behind the door" effect).

To conclude, our studies contribute to the issue of hypertext and cognition at two levels. First, we showed that in order to be effective, hypertext systems must support the flexibility of students' comprehension strategies. Second, we demonstrated the use of hypertext as a research tool. Our prototype hypertext system allowed us to obtain direct evidence about students' cognitive strategies when studying a set of historical documents. However, further research studies will be necessary in order to characterize the consequences of hypertext presentation on students' representation of document information.

ACKNOWLEDGMENTS

The research reported in this chapter was primarily supported by a grant from the Mellon Foundation. Additional funding was also provided by the United States Department of Education's Office of Educational Research and Improvement (OERI) to the Center for Student Learning, Learning Research and Development Center, and by a grant from the French Ministry of Foreign Affairs ("Lavoisier" Program) to the second author. The opinions expressed do not necessarily reflect the position or policy of the sponsors and no official endorsement should be inferred. The authors wish to thank Monik Favart, Mara Georgi, Julia Kushner, and Robert Mason for their contributions to this chapter, and Andrew Dillon for his useful comments on an earlier draft.

REFERENCES

Anderson, T. H., & Armbruster, B. B. (1984). Studying. In P. D. Pearson (Ed.), *Handbook of reading research* (pp. 657–680). New York: Longman.

Britt, M. A., Rouet, J.-F., Georgi, M. C., & Perfetti, C. A. (1994). Learning from history texts: From causal analysis to argument models. In I. L. Beck, G. Leinhardt, & C. Stainton (Eds.), *Teaching and learning in history* (pp. 47–84). Hillsdale, NJ: Lawrence Erlbaum Associates.

Charney, D. (in press). The impact of hypertext on processes of reading and writing. In S. J. Hilligoss & C. L. Selfe (Eds.), *Literacy and computers*. New York: MLA.

Dee-Lucas, D., & Larkin, J. H. (1992). *Text representation with traditional text and hypertext* (Technical Rep. H.P. #21). Carnegie Mellon University, Pittsburgh, PA: Department of Psychology.

Dillon, A. (1991). Reader's models of text structure: The case of academic articles. *International Journal of Man–Machine Studies, 35*, 913–925.

Dreher, M. J., & Guthrie, J. T. (1990). Cognitive processes in textbook chapter search tasks. *Reading Research Quarterly, 25*(4), 323–339.

Eco, U. (1992). Hypermedia for teaching and learning: A multimedia guide to the history of European civilization (MuG). In D. Lucarella, J. Nanard, M. Nanard, & P. Paolini (Eds.), *Proceedings of the 4th ACM Conference on Hypertext* (p. 288). New York: ACM Press.

Edwards, D., & Hardman, L. (1989). "Lost in hyperspace": Cognitive mapping and navigation in a hypertext environment. In R. McAleese (Ed.), *Hypertext: Theory into practice* (pp. 105–125). Oxford: Intellect.

Foltz, P. (1992). *Readers' comprehension and strategies in linear text and hypertext* (Tech. Rep. No. 93.01). Boulder, CO: Institute of Cognitive Science.

Foss, C. L. (1989). *Detecting lost users: Empirical studies on browsing hypertext* (Tech. Rep. No. 972). Nice, France: INRIA.

Goldman, S. R., & Saul, E. U. (1990). Flexibility in text processing: A strategy competition model. *Learning and Individual Differences, 2*(2), 181–219.

Gordon, S., Gustavel, J., Moore, J., & Hankey, J. (1988). The effect of hypertext on reader knowledge representation. *Proceedings of the 32nd Annual Meeting of the Human Factors Society, 32,* 296–300.

Guindon, R. (1990). Designing the design process: Exploiting opportunistic thoughts. *Human Computer Interaction 5,* 305–344.

Jacobson, R. A., & Spiro, R. J. (1992). Imagined conversations: The relevance of hypertext, pragmatism, and cognitive flexibility theory to the interpretation of "classic texts" in intellectual history. In D. Lucarella, J. Nanard, M. Nanard, & P. Paolini (Eds.), *Proceedings of the 4th ACM Conference on Hypertext* (pp. 131–140). New York: ACM Press.

Koved, L., & Shneiderman, B. (1986). Embedded menus: Selecting items in context. *Communications of the ACM, 29*(4), 312–318.

Lodevijks, H. (1982). Self-regulated versus teacher-provided sequencing of information in learning from text. In A. Flammer & W. Kintsch (Eds.), *Discourse processing* (pp. 509–520). Amsterdam: North Holland.

Marchionini, G., & Shneiderman, B. (1988). Finding facts versus browsing knowledge in hypertext systems. *IEEE Computer, 20,* 70–80.

McKnight, C., Dillon, A., & Richardson, J. (1990). A comparison of linear and hypertext formats in information retrieval. In R. McAleese & C. Green (Eds.), *Hypertext: State of the art* (pp. 10–19). Oxford: Intellect.

Mynatt, B. T., Leventhal, L. M., Instone, K., Farhat, J., & Rohlman, D. S. (1992). Hypertext or book: Which is better for answering questions? In P. Bauersfield, J. Benett, & G. Lynch (Eds.), *Proceedings of CHI '92* (pp. 19–25). New York: ACM Press.

Perfetti, C. A., Britt, M. A., & Georgi, M. C. (1995). *Text-based learning and reasoning: Studies in history.* Hillsdale, NJ: Lawrence Erlbaum Associates.

Reinking, D., & Rickman, S. S. (1990). The effects of computer-mediated text on the vocabulary learning and comprehension of intermediate grade readers. *Journal of Reading Behavior, 12*(4), 395–411.

Rouet, J.-F. (1990). Interactive text processing by inexperienced (hyper-) readers. In A. Rizk, N. Streitz, & J. André (Eds.), *Hypertexts: Concepts, systems, and applications* (pp. 250–260). Cambridge, England: Cambridge University Press.

Rouet, J.-F. (1992). Cognitive processing of hyperdocuments: When does nonlinearity help? In D. Lucarella, J. Nanard, M. Nanard, & P. Paolini (Eds.), *Proceedings of the 4th ACM Conference on Hypertext* (pp. 131–140). New York: ACM Press.

Rouet, J.-F., Britt, M. A., Mason, R. A., & Perfetti, C. A. (1992, November). *The use of hypertext system to study and reason about historical evidence.* Poster presented at ECHT '92, fourth ACM conference on hypertext, Milan, Italy.

Rouet, J.-F., Britt, M. A., Mason, R. A., & Perfetti, C. A. (1996). *Using multiple sources of evidence to reason about history.* Manuscript submitted for publication.

Rouet, J.-F., Favart, M., Britt, M. A., & Perfetti, C. A. (1994). *Representation and use of multiple documents by novice and expert history students*. Manuscript submitted for publication.

Shneiderman, B. (1987). User interface design and evaluation for an electronic encyclopedia. In G. Salvendy (Ed.), *Cognitive engineering and the design of human computer interaction and expert systems* (pp. 207–223). New York: Elsevier.

Shneiderman, B. (1989). Reflections on authoring, editing and managing hypertext. In E. Barrett (Ed.), *The society of text: Hypertext, hypermedia and the social construction of information* (pp. 115–131). Cambridge, MA: MIT Press.

Spiro, R. J., Feltovitch, P. J., Jacobson M. J., & Coulson, R. J. (1991). Cognitive flexibility, constructivism and hypertext: Random access instruction for advanced knowledge acquisition in ill-structured domains. *Educational Technology, 31*(5), 24–33.

Sweller, J., Chandler, P., Tierney, P., & Cooper, M. (1990). Cognitive load as a factor in the structuring of technical material. *Journal of Experimental Psychology: General, 119*, 176–192.

Tripp, S. D., & Robby, W. (1990). Orientation and disorientation in a hypertext lexicon. *Journal of Computer-based Instruction, 17*(4), 120–124.

Wagner, R. K., & Sternberg, R. J. (1987). Executive control in reading comprehension. In B. K. Britton & S. M. Glynn (Eds.), *Executive control processes in reading* (pp. 1–22). Hillsdale, NJ: Lawrence Erlbaum Associates.

Weyer, S. A. (1982). The design of a dynamic book for information search. *International Journal of Man-Machine Studies, 17*, 87–107.

Wineburg, S. S. (1991). Historical problem solving: A study of the cognitive processes used in the evaluation of documentary and pictorial evidence. *Journal of Educational Psychology, 83*, 73–87.

Wineburg, S. S. (1994). The cognitive representation of historical texts. In I. Beck & G. Leinhardt (Eds.), *Teaching and learning in history* (pp. 85–135). Hillsdale, NJ: Lawrence Erlbaum Associates.

Wineburg, S. S., & Wilson, S. M. (1991). Subject-matter knowledge in the teaching of history. In J. E. Brody (Ed.), *Advances in research on teaching: Vol. 2* (pp. 305–347). Greenwich, CT: JAI.

Wright, P. (1991). Cognitive overheads and prostheses: Some issues in evaluating hypertexts. In R. Furuta & D. Stotts (Eds.), *Proceedings of the Third ACM Conference on Hypertext* (pp. 1–12). New York: ACM Press.

Wright, P. (1993). To jump or not to jump: Strategy selection while reading electronic texts. In C. McKnight, A. Dillon, & J. Richardson (Eds.), *Hypertext: A psychological perspective* (pp. 137–152). Chichester, England: Ellis Horwood.

5

▼▼▼▼▼▼

Effects of Overview Structure on Study Strategies and Text Representations for Instructional Hypertext

Diana Dee-Lucas
Carnegie Mellon University

A major feature distinguishing hypertext from traditional text is the use of an access facility (i.e., browser, map, menu, etc.) to view text content. The access facility determines how readers interact with the text by defining how information is located and displayed. Accordingly, the effectiveness of a hypertext system is in part determined by the usability of the access facility. In the case of instructional hypertexts, the design of the access facility is especially critical because readers may have complex learning goals requiring the selection and integration of information from various text segments. In this case, readers need to develop a coherent representation of some or all of the hypertext content. As illustrated in this chapter, the design of the access facility can greatly influence readers' ability to locate and organize the required information in a manner appropriate to their learning goal.

Hypertext access facilities vary depending on the nature of the text content and the flexibility desired in permitting direct access to all or part of the available information. Common approaches include indices, content overviews, various search capabilities (such as word searches), and hot text (consisting of words in the text that can be selected to view additional content). Complex instructional hypertexts typically include more than one type of access facility. However, most instructional hypertexts include one or more content overviews indicating the information contained in the text (Jonassen, 1986). This type of overview can aid readers in developing effective study strategies, particularly in the case of texts allowing relatively free access to information (Halasz & Conklin, 1989; Heller, 1990; Jonassen, 1986; Tsai, 1988). One of the simplest types of overview consists of a structured or unstructured listing of the titles of the hypertext units (or nodes), which readers click on to display the unit content (Jonassen, 1986). The overview can specify the entire text content, or the units at a particular level of a text hierarchy (Billingsley, 1982; Weyer, 1982). This type of overview may or may not provide a structure for the text units through the organization and linking of the titles on the overview. For example, the titles can be organized into a hierarchy reflecting superordinate and subordinate relationships among units, or they can be a simple list (see Figs. 5.1a and 5.1b).

The current research investigated how the design of this type of content overview influences learning from instructional hypertext. It focused on the effects of overview structure on study strategies and text representations developed for different types of learning objectives. One set of studies compared hypertext studied with hierarchically structured and unstructured overviews. The second compared hypertext studied with more segmented and less segmented overviews (i.e., hypertext segmented into many small units or fewer larger units). In comparing these different hypertext formats, the experiments addressed the following issues. How does the degree of structure provided in the overview influence readers' ability to develop efficient and effective study strategies for meeting their learning objective? How does the overview structure affect qualitative and quantitative characteristics of the resulting text representation? And, does the degree of structure provided by the overview affect readers' judgments of the usability of the hypertext?

Research with traditional text suggests that the quality of readers' text representations depends on the degree to which they thoroughly process text details and interrelate the text content (Kintsch, 1986; van Dijk & Kintsch, 1983). Well-written traditional text facilitates text processing and the development of a coherent internal text representation through careful sequencing of related ideas and the use of familiar text organizations (Charney, 1987). These text features help readers develop a well-integrated and stable text representation. This has been shown in research with unstructured or poorly structured traditional text demonstrating that recall for these texts is often poorer than for well-structured texts (Brooks & Dansereau, 1983; Dee-Lucas & Larkin, 1990; Eylon & Reif, 1984; Kintsch & Yarbrough, 1982; Lorch & Lorch, 1985; Schwarz & Flammer, 1981). These results suggest that providing structure for hypertext units on the overview would facilitate the development of study strategies and internal text representations.

However, hypertext overviews differ from traditional text in the manner in which content structure is conveyed. Traditional text provides content structure through the use of rhetorical indicators of importance and organization within the text content. In contrast, a hypertext overview provides organizational information external to the units of the text proper (i.e., through the spatial layout and linking of the unit titles). This separation of organization and text likely requires extra processing in that readers must integrate these two sources of

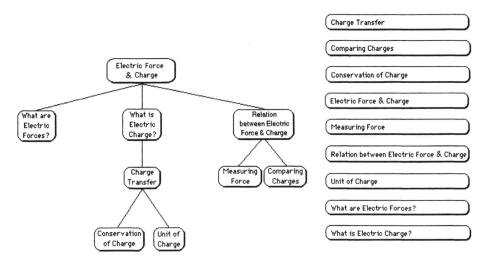

(a) Hierarchical overview. (b) List overview.

Electric Force and Charge

The electric force is a fundamental force of great importance. Because it is responsible for the interaction between atoms and molecules, it accounts ultimately for most phenomena studied in physics, and for all phenomena studied in chemistry and biology. Furthermore, it leads to an enormous range of practical applications in all technology and instrumentation. This text discusses the basic properties and implications of electric forces and electric charge.

I. What are Electric Forces?

The ancient Greeks as long ago as 600 B.C. knew that amber rubbed with wool acquires the property of attracting light objects, such as pieces of paper. This same phenomena can be demonstrated by running a rubber comb through dry hair, or against a carpet or a cat's fur--light objects will be attracted to the comb. In describing this property today, we say that the rubbed amber (or comb) exerts an electric force on other objects. If the object is light enough, we see it move in response to this force.

What is the nature of this electric force? It is not a force that requires physical contact between two objects. The paper scrap rises towards the comb without the comb touching it. It is not the force of gravity. Gravitational forces are very small unless one of the objects has an extremely large mass. The earth exerts a gravitational force on a scrap of paper, making it fall to the floor when dropped, but a comb is not massive enough to attract the paper through a gravitational force.

An interaction like that between the comb and paper (which is not an interaction through contact or a gravitational interaction), is called an electric interaction. It is due to an electric force created

(Next Page)

(c) First page of traditional text.

FIG. 5.1. Overviews for the two hypertexts and the first page of the traditional text. Adapted by permission from Dee-Lucas and Larkin (1995).

information (i.e., readers must incorporate the unit content within the overview structure). It also places additional emphasis on the structural information by presenting it in a manner that is distinct from the content itself. Furthermore, the manner in which the overview is used (i.e., to guide text search and study) also focuses attention on the overview titles and their organization because these form the basis on which readers decide what to select from the text.

The separation of content and structure with a hypertext overview and the manner in which the overview is used suggest that the overview organization may greatly influence hypertext study and learning. Because hypertext study is guided by the overview, providing structure in the overview may be particularly helpful in the development of goal-appropriate study strategies. By focusing attention on intraunit relationships, overview structure may also encourage the development of well-integrated text representations in situations where readers do not automatically try to interrelate the hypertext units. However, even if structured overviews enhance hypertext learning, it may not always be appropriate to provide such structure (Bergeron, 1994; Mayes, Kibby, & Anderson, 1990). Hypertext is designed to be a flexible information source that can be used for a variety of goals by students of varying backgrounds and skills. Because different structures are appropriate for different learners and learning goals, typically there is not one best structure for a body of information (Dee-Lucas & Larkin, 1990; Eylon & Reif, 1984). The research summarized in this chapter examines both the advantages and disadvantages of different types of overview structure in achieving different learning goals with simple instructional hypertext.

RESEARCH APPROACH AND GENERAL FINDINGS

The hypertexts developed for this research were similar in design to simple *chunked* or *node–link* hypertexts (see Jonassen, 1986). The text content was divided into information units that served as the hypertext nodes. Each unit had a title reflecting its content, and these titles were displayed on the overview providing access to the units. Readers clicked on the overview titles with a mouse to display the contents of the unit. The degree of structure provided by the overview was manipulated through the spatial arrangement of the titles (i.e., list-like vs. hierarchically organized) and the degree of segmentation of the text (i.e., a few large units providing little structure vs. many smaller units organized in a manner indicating main topics and subtopics).

For purposes of experimental control, the hypertexts used in this research contained few units. This limited the content that readers could select when using the different overviews so that representational differences could be examined for the same information studied with differently structured overviews. The hypertexts were also limited in the number of features provided and did not include many features typical of hypertext (e.g., hot text and word searches). This allowed examination of the effects of the overviews without the potential confounding that would result if readers had alternative methods for accessing the text.

The first two experiments examined the effects of the presence and absence of overview structure on learning from hypertext. They compared text review strategies and representations for hypertext studied with hierarchically structured and unstructured overviews, as well as a traditional linear text (studied on the computer). These comparisons were made when readers had a general learning goal of studying for an unspecified test (Experiment 1) and a specific goal of writing a text summary (Experiment 2). The third study examined the effects of different degrees of overview structure reflected in both unit size and organization. It compared unit selections and representations for more segmented hypertext having a few large units (with consequently little structure provided in the overview) and less segmented hypertext in which the units were divided into a greater number of smaller units (with a more highly structured overview providing a multilevel structure). These comparisons were made when readers had learning goals that varied in their compatibility with the text segmentation scheme. The results of these studies suggest the following conclusions:

- providing structure in the overview makes the hypertext easier to use, because (a) memory for unit locations on the overview is enhanced due to the more distinctive and meaningful spatial layout of structured overviews and (b) the organizational information aids the development of goal-appropriate study strategies
- differently structured overviews direct readers' attention to different aspects of the text, resulting in qualitative differences in the text representations
- overview structure and learning goal interact in determining the usability of a hypertext, but readers generally prefer hypertext over traditional printed text due to the direct information access provided by the overviews

A summary of the experiments and their results is presented next.

STRUCTURED AND UNSTRUCTURED HYPERTEXT

This research examined the effects of overview structure on text review and the resulting internal representation when readers had general and specific learning goals (see Dee-Lucas & Larkin, 1995, for a more complete report of this research). These experiments compared learning from three texts; a structured hypertext with a hierarchically structured overview (hierarchical overview), an unstructured hypertext with a menu-like list of the unit titles (list overview), and a traditional linear text presented on the computer. The traditional text contained the unit titles from the hypertext overviews as headings and subheadings within the text.

In the first experiment, readers studied these texts with a general learning goal of preparing for an unspecified test. Because this goal did not provide guidance for processing the text, it was expected that readers would rely on features of the text format and content in developing their study strategies. In this case, readers would use the information provided by the hypertext overview along with the unit content to decide what information was important to learn. Therefore, differences in overview format would have their greatest effect on the internal representation developed for the text content with this type of learning goal because the goal was not specific in its study requirements (i.e., does not direct attention to any particular information). Readers with the list overview were expected to have difficulty interrelating the units in the absence of either explicit structure or a specific learning objective around which to organize the content. However, readers with the hierarchically structured overview were expected to develop a well-integrated text representation based on the organizational information provided by the overview.

In the second experiment, readers were given the goal of preparing to write a summary of the text content. This task required readers to develop a coherent global representation, and thus assessed readers' ability to overcome potential difficulties in integrating information with the list overview. Research with traditional text has shown that readers are very flexible in generating strategies to overcome processing difficulties in order to meet a specific learning objective (Dee-Lucas & Larkin, 1990; Eylon & Reif, 1984; Kintsch, 1990). It was therefore expected that with this learning goal, readers with the list overview would develop a study strategy for organizing and integrating the text units, and write a summary comparable to readers with the hierarchical overview and traditional control text.

Method and Materials

The three experimental texts were identical in content. Each contained nine units. The hierarchical overview presented the unit titles in a hierarchy indicating the subordinate and superordinate relationships among the units. The list overview displayed the unit titles as an alphabetized list. The traditional text was formatted in the standard way with headings and subheadings that corresponded to the unit titles on the overview. The two overviews and the first page of the traditional text are presented in Fig. 5.1. Each hypertext unit and traditional text page was seen as a single computer screen display. The traditional text was segmented so that each page of the text filled one screen. Thus, one unit might be split between two pages, and one page might contain more than one unit, as would be the case with standard continuous text. This text was included as a control to compare the effects of structure when it was conveyed via an overview as opposed to being an inherent part of the text. The experimental texts were displayed on a Macintosh SE/30.

The subjects in the first experiment were 45 undergraduates who had completed not more than one semester of college-level physics. They were told to study the text in preparation for a test on its contents. In order to compare directly the internal representations developed with the two hypertexts and the traditional text, all readers first read all units in the same specified order and then reviewed any material they wanted to reread. This was done to ensure that all readers read the same material in the same initial sequence, in order to examine the effects of the different text formats on text review and learning for the same content. The order was specified in a message box at the bottom of the screen which provided the title of the unit that readers were to select during their first reading of the text. Each time readers finished a unit, a new message indicated which unit to select. When they had completed their study of the last unit, they saw a message indicating that they could either select any of the units for review or opt not to review. Readers with the traditional text format went through the text linearly, one screenful after the next, by clicking on a "next page" button. The order in which the units were presented matched the reading order specified in the message box for the hypertext units. After the last page, two new buttons appeared on the screen which allowed readers to go forward and backward to review.

After studying and reviewing a practice text and the experimental text, readers completed the following tasks. They summarized the main points of the text; provided a free recall of all the text content they could remember; completed a recall test for the unit names (for the overviews) or the corresponding text headings/subheadings (for the traditional text); and provided an open-ended evaluation of the usability of the text. For the summary, readers were asked to write up to 25 sentences including the main points of the text. The free recall required readers to write down everything they could remember from the text. The test for recall of unit titles and locations used a paper copy of the overview with the titles omitted. For the traditional control text, readers were given an outline corresponding to the headings and subheadings in the text (with the headings and subheadings omitted). The outline included the numbers and letters for the headings and subheadings (i.e., A,B,I,II, etc.) with appropriate spatial indentation in the outline. Readers were asked to recall the unit titles and, if possible, to indicate their location on the overview or outline.

In the second experiment, the materials and procedure were the same, but readers were given in advance the goal of preparing to write a summary of the main points of the text. The subjects were 63 undergraduates with the same limitations on college-level physics. These subjects had not participated in the first experiment. The instructions explained that the experiment was about how students summarize a computerized text, and that they would be writing a 10 to 15 sentence summary of what they read. They were told that the summary should include the ideas that were central to the text as a whole. The summaries were limited to 15 sentences rather than 25 (as in Experiment 1) to encourage readers to be more selective. As before, readers initially studied the material in the order specified and then reviewed any units. Afterward, they were given the same tasks as in Experiment 1.

Results

The main findings from the two experiments are presented below. Additional results are reported in Dee-Lucas and Larkin (1995). For all measures analyzed with an analysis of variance (ANOVA), all comparisons of the means were done with the Newman–Keuls test with $p < .05$.

Overview Usability

Readers found the hierarchical overview easier to use, regardless of learning goal, as indicated by the amount of time spent selecting units from the overviews. For both experiments, an ANOVA performed on the mean selection time spent on the overviews during their initial study showed that readers spent longer on the list than on the hierarchical overview. In Experiment 1, readers spent an average of 5.49 seconds on the list overview and 4.18 seconds on the hierarchical overview, $F(1, 28) = 5.36$, $MSE = 2.38$, $p < .028$. In Experiment 2, readers spent 5.40 seconds on the list overview and 4.26 seconds on the hierarchical overview, $F(1, 40) = 4.26$, $MSE = 3.19$, $p < .045$. This effect was found in the review times as well, with readers again spending more time in unit selection with the list overview. Thus, the hierarchical overview was easier to use in deciding what to review as well as for initial reading.

Memory for Overview Titles and Organization

The ability to recall the unit titles did not differ between overviews, but readers with the hierarchical overview were better able to recall the locations of the titles they remembered. In Experiment 1, the mean proportion of titles recalled was .39 for the hierarchical overview, .36 for the list overview, and .13 for the traditional text. Readers recalled significantly more titles with the hypertexts than with the traditional text, with no difference between hypertexts, $F(2, 42) = 15.08$, $MSE = .020$, $p < .001$. However, the mean proportion of title locations recalled (for correctly recalled titles) was significantly greater for the hierarchical overview than for the list overview or traditional text, $F(2, 37) = 6.76$, $MSE = .012$, $p < .003$. The means were .21 for the hierarchical overview, .11 for the list overview, and .05 for the traditional text.

This same pattern of results was obtained in Experiment 2. Readers with both hypertexts recalled significantly more titles than readers with the traditional text, $F(2, 60) = 8.38$, $MSE = .04$, $p < .001$. Traditional text readers recalled a mean of .18 titles compared to .41 for the hierarchical hypertext and .40 for the list hypertext. The proportion of recalled titles whose location was accurately recalled was again significantly greater for the hierarchical hypertext than for the other texts, $F(2, 51) = 8.59$, $MSE = .11$, $p < .001$. These proportions were .69 for the hierarchical hypertext, .26 for the list hypertext, and .44 for the traditional text.

This improved memory for title locations may have contributed to the faster unit selection times with the hierarchical overview. Readers may have been able to locate information more easily on the hierarchical overview because they were better able to remember the spatial layout of the titles, and therefore did not have to search the overview for units. Additionally, the organizational information provided by the hierarchical overview may have enabled readers to select units for review more quickly by helping them decide what to review.

Unit Review Strategies

The analyses of unit review suggested that readers with the list hypertext had more difficulty developing a review strategy with the general learning goal in the first experiment than with the specific goal in Experiment 2. Additionally, the nature of the review strategies differed for the two hypertexts. The hierarchical hypertext resulted in repeated skimming of units, whereas the list hypertext produced longer initial review times that decreased with repeated review. Text review strategies were characterized in terms of the number of readers reviewing, and the unit review times.

Number of Readers Reviewing. In Experiment 1, a z test indicated that significantly fewer readers reviewed the list hypertext than the other two texts, suggesting that these readers may have had difficulty deciding what to review, thus opting not to review. The percentage of readers reviewing was .93 for the traditional text, .87 for the hierarchical hypertext, and .47 for the list hypertext. However, in Experiment 2, there were no differences in the proportion of readers reviewing each text. These proportions were .95 for the list hypertext, .90 for the hierarchical hypertext, and .95 for the traditional control text. Thus, readers of the list hypertext were better able to develop a review strategy with the specific goal of summarizing than with the general goal of studying for an unspecified test.

Review Times. Review times were analyzed with a multiple regression on the logarithm of the time spent by each reader reviewing each unit (for those units reviewed). The data for the traditional text were not included in the analysis because search times (i.e., skimming through successive screens of text) cannot be separated from individual unit review times for this text. The independent variables in the regression analysis for Experiment 1 included unit (the unit reviewed) and overview structure (hierarchical or list hypertext). Subjects were also entered as categorical variables to account for individual differences in study time. The coefficients for the regression analysis (without the subject coefficients) are shown in Table 5.1. Because each unit was entered as a categorical variable, Table 5.1 shows a separate coefficient for all nine units.

The coefficient for overview structure indicates longer review times for the list hypertext than for the hierarchical hypertext. The estimated unit review times based on the regression coefficients were 8.70 seconds (hierarchical hypertext) and 27.45

TABLE 5.1
Parameter Estimates and Standard Errors for a Regression Model of the
Log of the Review Times (in Seconds) from Experiment 1

Variable	Coefficient	Standard error	P value
Intercept	1.189	—	—
Overview structure	−.250	.052	.01
Unit 1	.126	.115	.28
Unit 2	.071	.112	.53
Unit 3	.055	.104	.60
Unit 4	−.031	.111	.78
Unit 5	.057	.088	.52
Unit 6	.151	.085	.08
Unit 7	−.317	.097	.01
Unit 8	.089	.106	.41
Unit 9	−.200	.143	.17

Note. $R^2 = .67$; multiple $R = .82$. Adapted by permission from Dee-Lucas and Larkin (1995).

seconds (list hypertext). Thus, readers who reviewed the list hypertext spent a relatively long time on the units they reread, suggesting that they were not skimming for information but were rereading the entire unit. The coefficients for units in Table 5.1 indicate that some units were reviewed longer than others, reflecting differences among units in characteristics such as length and syntactic complexity.

In Experiment 2, readers reviewed units multiple times, and exhibited different review strategies with repeated study of the units. The regression analysis for these review times included the effects of unit and overview structure, as in Experiment 1. Additionally, because readers in Experiment 2 often reviewed units several times (repeatedly going back to the same unit), variables for review episode and the interaction between overview structure and review episode were also included. Finally, subjects were entered as categorical variables. The coefficients for the regression model (excluding the subject coefficients) are in Table 5.2.

Although the main effects were significant, the coefficient for the interaction between overview structure and review episode indicates that the effect of overview structure varied with the number of times the unit had been read. Figure 5.2 shows the estimated review times for this interaction based on the regression analysis. On the first review, times were longer for the list than the hierarchical hypertext, as in Experiment 1. However, review times decreased with multiple readings of units in the list hypertext, whereas readers with the hierarchical hypertext spent approximately the same amount of time on each rereading of a unit. As in Experiment 1, the coefficients for units (Table 5.2) show that readers spent more time on some units than on others.

The differences between hypertexts in review strategies suggest that readers with the list hypertext were less willing to casually skim units. This may be

TABLE 5.2
Parameter Estimates and Standard Errors for a Regression Model of the
Log of the Review Times (in Seconds) from Experiment 2

Variable	Coefficient	Standard error	P value
Intercept	1.162	—	—
Overview Structure (OS)	−.106	.041	.01
Unit 1	.204	.048	.01
Unit 2	.065	.051	.20
Unit 3	.049	.053	.36
Unit 4	−.036	.056	.53
Unit 5	−.212	.060	.01
Unit 6	.241	.048	.01
Unit 7	−.229	.061	.01
Unit 8	−.054	.058	.35
Unit 9	−.029	.052	.57
Review episode (RE)	−.078	.027	.01
RE × OS	.059	.027	.03

Note. $R^2 = .39$; multiple $R = .63$. Adapted by permission from Dee-Lucas and Larkin (1995).

related to the greater difficulty finding units on this overview. Readers may have wanted to ensure that they would not have to reread units several times by processing the units thoroughly on the first review. Another possibility is that readers with the hierarchical overview had a better global representation of the text and therefore were better able to read selectively within the unit, thus resulting in shorter review times.

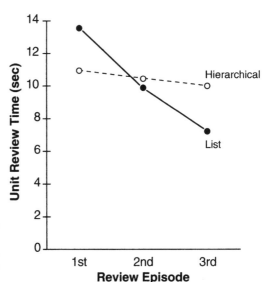

FIG. 5.2. Estimated review times (based on Table 5.2) for the two hypertexts during the first, second, and third review episodes. Adapted by permission from Dee-Lucas and Larkin (1995).

Text Representations

The analyses of the free recalls indicated that there were no quantitative differences among the texts in representations developed for either learning goal. However, there were qualitative differences reflected in readers' ability to write an unanticipated summary. With the general learning goal, readers with the list hypertext included fewer main ideas in their summaries than readers with the two structured texts.

Text recall was examined by analyzing the text content into its component propositions, and scoring the free recalls for the number of propositions recalled (see Dee-Lucas & Larkin, 1995, for more details). An ANOVA indicated no significant differences among the texts in the proportion of text propositions recalled in either experiment. To examine breadth of recall, an ANOVA was run on the proportion of text units from which at least one proposition was recalled. For both experiments, there was no difference between the hypertexts in breadth of recall, although in Experiment 1, both hypertexts resulted in recall from more units than did the traditional text, $F(2, 42) = 4.93$, $MSE = .015$, $p < .012$.

Although there were no quantitative differences in text recall, there were differences in the ability to summarize the main points when readers had the general learning goal. In Experiment 1, summaries of both the hierarchical hypertext and the traditional text contained significantly more main ideas than did summaries of the list hypertext, $F(2, 41) = 3.91$, $MSE = .027$, $p < .028$. These main ideas had been identified in another study in which readers had been asked to select the main ideas from a printed version of the text. The fact that readers with the list hypertext recalled as much content as readers with the structured texts, but wrote poorer text summaries, suggests that the list hypertext units were processed as independent text segments. The mean proportion of main ideas in the summaries was .63 for the traditional text, .67 for the hierarchical hypertext, and .51 for the list hypertext. In contrast, in Experiment 2, there were no differences among texts in the proportion of main ideas in the summaries. These means were .49 (traditional text), .57 (hierarchical hypertext), and .56 (list hypertext). Thus, readers with the list hypertext were able to integrate the text units in a manner similar to readers with structured texts when this was required by the study goal.

Although readers in Experiment 2 were told prior to studying the text that they would be summarizing the central ideas, their summaries included fewer main ideas than did the summaries of readers in the first experiment. This may be due to how they interpreted the summary instructions. In the second experiment the readers were told that they would be writing a summary of the ideas central to the text as a whole. However, their study strategies involved repeated review of the entire text rather than focusing on particular text units. This suggests that readers tried to write a 15-sentence summary that was representative of all of the text content, rather than including only the more important central ideas. Thus the decrease in the number of important ideas in the summaries from

Experiment 2 most likely reflects an attempt to write a summary of the entire text, rather than selecting main points.

Readers' Subjective Evaluations

After completing all other measures, readers indicated whether they thought the experimental text they had studied was more difficult or easier to use than standard printed text, and why. Readers generally felt that the hierarchical hypertext was easy to use with both learning goals, but evaluated the list hypertext more positively with the summary goal. Reader evaluations of text formats expressed as proportions are presented in Table 5.3. In order to determine whether readers indicating a preference were in agreement in their judgments, a multiway frequency analysis was run on these data for each experiment (excluding readers with no preference). Both analyses indicated that the best fitting model was the saturated model including the interaction between text format and reader evaluation.

For each experiment, a series of z tests were run on the proportion of readers evaluating each text as easier to use than printed text. In Experiment 1, significantly more readers preferred the hierarchical hypertext than preferred the traditional control text (compared to printed text), with no difference between these two texts and the list hypertext. In Experiment 2, significantly more readers of both hypertexts preferred these texts to printed text than did readers with the traditional control text. For the hierarchical hypertext, ease of determining information organization and easy access to information provided by the overview

TABLE 5.3

Readers' Judgments of the Difficulty of Using the Experimental Texts Relative to Traditional Printed Text: Proportion of Readers Giving Each Response

	Experiment 1		
Text format	More difficult	Easier	No difference or no opinion
Hierarchical hypertext	.13	.73	.13
List hypertext	.47	.40	.13
Traditional control text	.47	.33	.20
	Experiment 2		
Text format	More difficult	Easier	No difference or no opinion
Hierarchical hypertext	.33	.57	.10
List hypertext	.33	.52	.14
Traditional control text	.62	.14	.24

Note.   Adapted by permission from Dee-Lucas and Larkin (1995).

were given as reasons for preferring this text in both experiments. Readers with the list hypertext also cited easy access to information in justifying their preference in both experiments. However, in Experiment 2, these readers also indicated that the hypertext facilitated information organization, even though the list overview did not provide organizational information. It may be that with the summary goal, readers devoted more effort to organizing the information units, and found the overview helpful in presenting a listing of the content for organization.

A series of z tests were also run on the proportion of readers indicating that their experimental text was more difficult. In Experiment 1, these tests showed that significantly more readers judged the traditional control text and list hypertext as more difficult than the printed text relative to these judgments for the hierarchical hypertext. In Experiment 2, there were no significant differences among the three texts. The main disadvantages cited for the list hypertext in Experiment 1 were physical limitations of using a computer (e.g., must sit in the same position, greater eye strain, etc.) and organizational difficulties in structuring the information (e.g., harder to organize recall and text loses the flow of normal text). Readers with the list hypertext in Experiment 2 also indicated that they were bothered by the physical limitations of reading from a computer, but did not indicate that they had organizational difficulties. These readers may have felt that they could adequately organize the content when given a specific goal such as summarizing, but felt a need for some organization inherent to the text presentation with the general learning goal. With the hierarchical hypertext, too few readers in Experiment 1 indicated that this text was difficult to characterize their responses. In Experiment 2, readers with the hierarchical hypertext based their negative judgment on the lack of features typically found in printed texts (e.g., inability to take notes or highlight, lack of illustrations, etc.).

Summary

The results of these experiments indicate that providing structure in a hypertext overview can enhance its usability by facilitating unit selection. Regardless of the study goal, readers spent less time selecting units from the hierarchical overview than from the list overview. This may have been related to the fact that readers were better able to recall the title locations with the hierarchical overview. This overview may have facilitated memory for title locations due to its more distinctive and meaningful spatial layout. The titles on the hierarchical overview formed a two-dimensional array, whereas the titles on the list overview were simply higher or lower in the list, and thus, less spatially distinct. Additionally, the titles on the hierarchical overview were positioned in a meaningful way with related topics grouped together, so that recall of the location of one title may have prompted recall for the location of related titles. In the case of text review, the organizational information provided by the hierarchical overview may have further facilitated unit selection by helping readers decide what to review.

Overview structure also facilitated the development of text review strategies when readers did not have a specific learning goal. With the general learning goal, fewer readers with the list overview reviewed than with the hierarchical overview. In contrast, with the specific goal of summarizing, all readers reviewed both hypertexts extensively. This suggests that it was easier for readers to develop a study strategy for the list hypertext when they had a specific goal for organizing the units. This is consistent with readers' comments indicating that they had difficulty organizing the text units with the general learning goal, but not the specific goal.

There were no quantitative differences in the text representations developed with the two hypertexts, but there were qualitative differences with the general learning goal. Readers of the list hypertext had more trouble generating or recalling the main points than did readers of the other texts. This may have been due to both the lack of organization for the units and the decrease in text review relative to the other texts. However, readers of the list hypertext wrote summaries comparable to those of the structured texts when given this as the study goal. This indicates that readers do not automatically develop a well-integrated representation for hypertext units when the overview lacks structure, but can do so if required by the study goal. The increase in review of the list hypertext with the summary goal may have reflected additional text processing needed to determine how the units were interrelated in order to write a summary for this text.

Readers' subjective evaluations of the usability of the overviews were similar in both experiments. Readers thought the hierarchical hypertext provided easy access to information and aided in determining information organization. Readers of the list hypertext also indicated that it provided easy access to information. However, they felt that they had organizational difficulties studying this text for the general learning goal, but that the overview provided useful organizational information for the summary goal. It may be that readers found the list overview helpful in indicating the text topics available for summarizing.

MORE AND LESS SEGMENTED HYPERTEXT

This research examined the effects of degree of text segmentation on study strategies and text representations developed for hypertext studied with different learning goals. It examined the potential trade-off between study efficiency and incidental learning for more and less segmented hypertext when the study goals matched or mismatched the segmentation scheme presented on the overview.

In a more segmented hypertext, the text content is divided into many relatively small units. A more segmented hypertext indicates more precisely the location of specific information, and is correspondingly more complex. In a less segmented hypertext, the text content is divided into fewer larger units. This results in an overview that is simpler, but less specific in indicating where particular information is located.

A more segmented overview allows readers to quickly find information, but decreases the amount of text material read or skimmed because less text search is required. Thus, there may be a trade-off in study efficiency and breadth of learning in the amount of incidental content read and recalled with more segmented overviews. However, the degree to which more segmented overviews facilitate readers' ability to meet their study goals and decrease incidental learning would depend on the extent to which the location of the needed information was also apparent with a less segmented overview. In cases where the goal-related content is obvious with both less and more segmented overviews, differences in learning efficiency and text representations would be expected to be smaller because the ability to find the needed information would not differ between overviews. However, because the units in a less segmented hypertext contain more information, readers with this hypertext would still have to skim through more content within the units to locate the specific information needed. Thus, there may be more incidental learning with less segmented hypertext even when the location of the needed information is readily apparent on the overview. This study compared study strategies and text recall with more and less segmented hypertexts when readers had (1) a study goal compatible with the more segmented overview (i.e., the location of the target content was obvious), but incompatible with the less segmented overview (i.e., it was not clear which unit contained the target content), and (2) a goal compatible with both text segmentations.

Method and Materials

Two versions of a hypertext were developed, a more segmented hypertext containing many small units and a less segmented hypertext containing fewer larger units. The overviews for these hypertexts are shown in Fig. 5.3. The content of the two hypertexts was identical. For the more segmented version, the material was divided into 22 units organized into three levels of detail on the overview. For the less segmented overview, the units at the third level of detail were combined with their superordinate second-level units, resulting in nine units. The units were combined by adding the third level units to the end of the corresponding second level units, so that the combined unit read as continuous text. Whereas all units in the more segmented hypertext were no longer than one screen of text, some units in the less segmented hypertext contained two or three screens of text due to their greater length. Readers studied the texts by clicking on the unit titles on the overviews. The experiment was run on a Macintosh SE/30.

The two learning goals consisted of a problem solving task (solve task) and a task in which readers had to find the definitions for three terms (information

(a) More segmented hypertext.

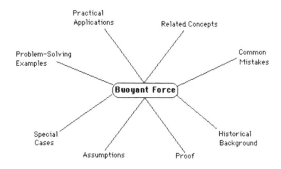

(b) Less segmented hypertext.

FIG. 5.3.   Overviews for the more and less segmented hypertexts.

location task). The solve task required readers to determine the buoyant force on a partially filled object submerged in a fluid. In order to solve the problem, readers had to understand how to compute buoyancy, and select the relevant volume from two that were provided in the problem. The solve task matched the segmentation scheme of both hypertexts because the relevant text units were readily apparent on both overviews. The information location task required readers to find the definitions for three terms. This was basically a search task in that these definitions were provided in the text. However, in some cases, the terms were defined both in general terms and more specifically in different portions of the text so readers had to determine if they had located the most specific definition before ending their search. The information location task was compatible with the segmentation scheme for the more segmented overview (in which the unit titles of the relevant third-level units matched the terms to be defined), but not the less segmented overview. In the latter case, the titles of the combined second level units did not suggest where the definitions might be located.

For both study goals, the content needed to complete the tasks was contained in the third-level units of the more segmented hypertext. In the less segmented text, this information occurred at the end of the second-level units, because these units were formed by combining second- and third-level units from the more segmented hypertext. In cases where a less segmented text unit consisted of two or three text screens, readers needed to read or skim all of the unit's text screens to find the target content located near the end of the unit.

The subjects were 64 undergraduates who had completed not more than two semesters of college level physics. Each reader studied a practice hypertext, and then one of the two versions of the hypertext twice, once with the solve task and once with the information location task as the study goal. The order of presentation of the tasks was counterbalanced. Readers were given the learning goal prior to studying the text. They were allowed to select any units they wanted to read in any order, and review the units as often as they liked. They were also able to take notes at any time by clicking on a button which displayed a screen on which they could type notes. After each study of the text, readers completed the study goal using any notes they had taken. After the second study of the text, they completed several additional measures. These included a free recall of all the text content they could recall; a recall test for the unit names and their location on the overview (using the overviews with the unit names excluded, as in the previous experiments); and a questionnaire evaluating the usability of their hypertext.

Results

The main findings relating to the issues raised in this chapter are presented next.

Efficiency in Using the Overviews

With both learning goals, readers spent more time selecting units from the more segmented than from the less segmented overview, probably reflecting the fact that there were a greater number of choices. However, readers became more efficient with practice at using the more segmented overview, selecting fewer units in completing the second task.

Unit Selection Time.   Because different readers selected different units (i.e., unit selection was not constrained as in the earlier research), unit selection times were analyzed with a multiple regression analysis on the logarithm of the time spent by each reader selecting each unit (for those units selected). The variables in the analysis included task (information location vs. solve), text segmentation (more or less segmented), serial position (whether the selection was the first, second, third, etc., from the overview), and order (whether the reader was completing the first or second task). Based on preliminary analyses, the interaction between task and serial position, and order and serial position were also added. Subjects were entered as categorical variables. The coefficients for the analysis (excluding subject variables) are shown in Table 5.4.

The coefficient for text segmentation indicated that unit selection times were longer for the more segmented overview. The longer unit selection times for this overview most likely reflect additional time needed to select a unit from a larger set of alternatives. There was no Text Segmentation × Task interaction, even though the content needed for the information location task was clearly evident only on the more segmented overview (with the location of information for the solve task obvious on both overviews). It may be that the expected increase in selection time for the information location task with the less segmented hypertext was not large enough to offset the overall longer selection times for the more segmented hypertext.

The negative coefficient for task showed that readers took longer to select units for the information location task, most likely because this task consisted of three subtasks (i.e., finding three definitions). The interaction between task and serial position indicated that selection times decreased more rapidly for the information location task than for the solve task with repeated use of the overview. This suggests that the ability to locate the definitions for the information location task was aided by experience using the overviews. The Order × Serial Position interaction showed that unit selection times decreased more rapidly with repeated use on the first task than on the second task. This was due to the fact that completing the first task facilitated the location of information needed for the second task, so repeated use of the overview on the second task did not significantly improve information location.

TABLE 5.4
Parameter Estimates and Standard Errors for a Regression Model of the
Log of the Unit Selection Times (in Seconds) from Experiment 3

Variable	Coefficient	Standard error	P value
Intercept	.651	—	—
Text segmentation	.038	.011	.01
Order	−.021	.022	.34
Serial position	−.007	.002	.01
Task	−.051	.018	.01
Task × Serial position	.004	.001	.01
Order × Serial position	.004	.002	.01

Note. $R^2 = .18$; multiple $R = .43$.

Number of Units Selected. An analysis of the number of units selected with the two overviews indicated that the ability to find the needed information improved with repeated use of the more segmented overview, but not the less segmented overview. An ANOVA on the number of units selected at least once by each subject for each task indicated significant main effects for text segmentation, $F(1, 60) = 4.32$, $MSE = 11.28$, $p < .042$, and task, $F(1, 60) = 4.36$, $MSE = 7.11$, $p < .041$. Significant interaction effects were found for Order $\times$ Task, $F(1, 60) = 23.09$, $MSE = 7.11$, $p < .001$; Text Segmentation $\times$ Task, $F(1, 60) = 5.85$, $MSE = 7.11$, $p < .019$; and Order $\times$ Text Segmentation $\times$ Task, $F(1, 60) = 13.05$, $MSE = 7.11$, $p < .001$. More units were selected from the more segmented than from the less segmented hypertext, reflecting the fact that this text had more units for selection. However, the three-way interaction between order, task, and text segmentation indicates that the main effect of text segmentation depended on other variables. With the more segmented hypertext, the number of units selected was influenced only by task order. Readers selected more units for each task when it was first as opposed to second, indicating that readers became more efficient with experience in using this overview for both learning goals. The mean number of units selected for the information location task was 8.3 when it was first, and 3.9 when it was second. For the solve task, readers selected 8.1 units when the task was first, and 4.5 units when it was second. However, with the less segmented overview, there was no significant difference in the number of units selected for either task when it was first and second. The mean number of units selected for the information location task was 6.0 when it was performed first, and 6.1 when it was completed second. For the solve task, these means were 4.5 and 3.3; the difference was not statistically significant. Thus, experience with this overview did not increase study efficiency. One reason may have been that the larger size of the units made it difficult for readers to recall where they had encountered the information needed for the second task while working on the first task. Another possibility is that the longer length of the units may have encouraged readers to skim for the information needed. They therefore had to reread units when given a new task because they had not thoroughly covered all of the content on the initial reading.

Memory for Overview Titles and Organization

The analyses of readers' memory for the overviews indicated that the more segmented overview resulted in recall of more titles overall, but poorer recall of the titles common to both overviews (the first- and second-level titles). The more segmented overview also resulted in better recall of the locations of the titles on the overview.

An ANOVA on the total number of titles recalled indicated that readers of the more segmented overview recalled more titles, $F(1, 60) = 56.35$, $MSE = 7.37$, $p < .001$, but a smaller proportion of available titles, $F(1, 60) = 7.60$, $MSE = .03$, $p < .008$, than readers with the less segmented overview. The mean number of titles recalled from the more segmented overview was 10.3 (47% of available titles); for the less segmented overview this mean was 5.2 titles (58% of the titles). In order to determine whether readers tended to recall titles from the same location on the overviews, an ANOVA was run on recall of the titles common to both overviews. These consisted of all titles excluding the third-level units which appeared only on the more segmented overview. The analysis indicated that more of the common titles were recalled with the less segmented hypertext, $F(1, 60) = 12.36, MSE = 2.91, p < .001$. Readers of the more segmented hypertext recalled 3.7 (41%) of these titles, compared to the 5.2 or 58% with the less segmented hypertext. The fact that higher level unit titles were better recalled with the less segmented overview suggests that the more segmented overview focused attention on the third-level units.

An ANOVA on the proportion of unit titles recalled whose location was also correctly recalled indicated better location memory with the more segmented overview, $F(1, 60) = 7.41, MSE = .04, p < .009$. Readers with the more segmented overview recalled .84 of the title locations; readers of the less segmented overview recalled .70 of the locations. The same analysis conducted for the common titles also indicated better location memory with the more segmented overview, $F(1, 60) = 11.58, MSE = .06, p < .001$. More segmented readers recalled a mean of .90 of these locations compared to .70 for the less segmented hypertext. As in the previously reported research, the better location recall may be related to the more distinctive spatial layout of the more segmented overview. Additionally, the greater number of titles provided more recall prompts for title location because recalling the location of one title could aid in recall of the location of related titles.

Unit Selection Strategies

An examination of the types of units selected with the two hypertexts indicated that readers with the more segmented overview were less likely to select units that were irrelevant to the learning goal. This was examined by categorizing each unit according to whether it contained target (goal relevant) information, related (but not required) information, and irrelevant information for each learning goal. The number of readers selecting each unit within each category was totaled and averaged over the number of units in the category (which varied with text segmentation). A multiway frequency analysis was run on the average number of readers selecting each category of unit (averaged over units within the category) for each task in each order, and with each hypertext. The best fitting model included the main effects of text segmentation and unit category, and their interaction, $\chi^2(18, N = 219) = 14.74, p < .680$.[1] There was no difference between the hypertexts in the selection of target and related units, but readers with the

---

[1]A multiway frequency analysis fits a loglinear model to categorical data. The loglinear model expresses the logarithm of the expected cell frequencies as an additive function of main effects and interactions, in a manner similar to the typical analysis of variance model. A nonsignificant chi-square indicates that there is not a reliable difference between the observed and predicted values based on the model.

more segmented hypertext were less likely to select irrelevant units. This was true even when the analysis was rerun on a subset of the data for two irrelevant units that were the same on both overviews (i.e., did not have lower level units in the more segmented hypertext). Because these units were identical in their presentation on the two overviews, the ability to determine the type of information they contained should have been similar for both hypertexts. However, readers were more likely to select these units when they were presented on the less segmented hypertext, even though their titles indicated that they were not likely to be relevant to the learning goal. It may be that when the overview contains relatively few units, readers are willing to view most or all of the units because the cost of accessing all units is low. When readers have to select from among many units, they may be more selective because it is not practical to view everything. It may also be the case that readers with a less segmented hypertext are less sure that they have located the needed information (in part because they must scan larger units), so they tend to check more tangential units to make sure they have all of the information they need.

Because the more segmented overview provided three levels of structure, readers had an opportunity to either follow a path to the target content (by selecting superordinate units prior to selecting the target unit) or go directly to the most specific unit containing the target information. To examine in greater detail the selection strategies of readers with the more segmented overview, each reader's strategy was characterized according to the location of the unit selected first. Readers selecting a third-level unit first (rather than following a path from second- to third-level information) were classified as having a specific first selection strategy. Readers selecting second-level units prior to related subordinate third-level units were classified as having a general first selection strategy. These classifications were made for each of the four overview branches containing both second- and third-level units. Any cases in which reader strategies were ambiguous were excluded from the data. A multiway frequency analysis was performed on the number of readers displaying specific first and general first strategies for each of the four multilevel branches in the more segmented hypertext. The best fitting model included the main effect of selection strategy, $\chi^2(6, N = 95) = 8.57, p < .20$, with more readers using a specific first strategy than a general first strategy. These findings indicate that readers with a more segmented overview tend to go directly to the most specific units containing the information they need rather than follow a path through superordinate units to specific units. This strategy is more efficient, but results in exposure to less text content overall than if readers selected related higher level units as well.

Overview Effectiveness

Although most of the 64 readers completed the learning tasks successfully, more errors occurred with the less segmented hypertext, due to difficulty in locating the target information. There were a total of 12 errors on the information location task, and 8 on the solve task (excluding arithmetic errors). The effects of text segmentation on task performance were analyzed with a multiway frequency analysis on the number of readers completing each task correctly. For the solve task, the variables included were text segmentation (more or less segmented) and task order (whether the task was first or second). For the information location task, the analysis included the additional variable of target term (i.e., which of the three terms were to be defined). The analysis for the solve task indicated no differences due to either text segmentation or task order. This would be expected given that the location of the problem-related information was readily apparent with both overviews. However, the best fitting model for the information location task included the main effect of text segmentation, $\chi^2(20, N = 192) = 6.62, p < .998$. More errors were made with the less segmented text (a total of 10) than with the more segmented text (a total of 2). Of the errors made with the less segmented hypertext, 80% were due to readers not finding the target content because they did not read to the end of multiscreen units where the term was located (i.e., they selected the correct unit, but only read the beginning of the unit without going to subsequent screens where the target content was located). These readers either gave up without responding, or based their answer on more general information occurring early in the unit. Thus, the ability to find the target terms for the information location task with the less segmented hypertext depended on the readers' persistence and thoroughness in checking the text content. The rest of the errors involved incorrect recall or interpretation of an equation, or responses unrelated to the text content.

Text Representations

Although the more and less segmented hypertexts resulted in different study strategies, there were no differences between texts in the overall amount of information recalled. There were, however, differences in which parts of the text were recalled. The less segmented hypertext enhanced recall of the more superordinate text content occurring at the beginning of the units for this text (located in the second-level units of the more segmented text). These recall differences are consistent with differences in study strategies indicating that the more segmented hypertext focused attention on third-level text units.

The free recalls were scored using the same method described for the earlier experiments. An ANOVA on the proportion of text propositions recalled indicated a significant effect due to task order, $F(1, 60) = 4.68, MSE = .001, p < .034$, but no effect due to text segmentation. Readers recalled more when the information location task was performed first than when the solve task was first. An ANOVA also indicated no differences between texts in the number of units recalled (i.e., the number of units from which at least one proposition was remembered).

Because readers focused on different portions of the text during text study, the free recall data were reanalyzed in terms of which segments of the text were recalled. Each recall was scored for the number of propositions recalled from third-level units and second-level units, as defined on the more segmented overview. Although the combined units of the less segmented overview were not divided into second and third levels, the free recalls were scored according to these unit divisions in order to examine incidental learning of information contained in the second-level units of the more segmented hypertext. (This information was located at the beginning of the combined second-level units of the less segmented hypertext.) Because the second-level units of the more segmented hypertext did not contain target information for the learning goals, readers tended not to select these. However, readers with the less segmented text were required to skim this content in searching for the target information located at the end of larger combined second- and third-level units that comprised this hypertext. An ANOVA was run on the proportion of each subject's total recall consisting of propositions from second-level units (as defined by the more segmented hypertext). The results indicated a significant main effect of text segmentation, $F(1, 60) = 7.74$, $MSE = .029$, $p < .007$. A significantly greater proportion of recall from the less segmented hypertext consisted of information from these second-level units. For the more segmented hypertext, .09 of the recall consisted of propositions from these units, whereas for readers of the less segmented hypertext, this proportion was .21. Thus, the two overviews produced qualitative differences in the location of the text content that was recalled, which were consistent with differences in readers' attention during text study.

Readers' Subjective Evaluations

As in the previous experiments, readers were asked to indicate whether they thought the hypertext was more difficult or easier to study than traditional printed text, and why. Readers overwhelmingly preferred both hypertexts over traditional printed text. The responses were classified into easier, harder, or no preference, and a multiway frequency analysis was run on the number of responses in each category for each hypertext and task order. These data are shown in Table 5.5. The results indicated no effects due to either variable, with readers judging both hypertexts as easier to use than standard printed text, $\chi^2(9, N = 64) = 4.03$, $p < .909$. The most common reason given for preferring the hypertexts was that they facilitated information location.

Readers were also asked if they had difficulty determining where task-related information was located. As expected, readers with the less segmented hypertext had more difficulty than readers with the more segmented hypertext. Responses were classified into those stating that the location of the needed information was not obvious, obvious, and mixed responses (see Table 5.5). A multiway frequency analysis performed on the number of responses in each category for each hypertext and each task order indicated an interaction between hypertext and response, $\chi^2(6, N = 63) = 6.09$, $p < .413$. Readers of the less segmented hypertext indicated more difficulty in locating information than readers with the more segmented hypertext. However, most readers of the less segmented hypertext gave a mixed

TABLE 5.5
Readers' Judgments of the Difficulty of Using the Experimental Texts Relative
to Traditional Printed Text: Proportion of Readers Giving Each Response

Usability judgments			
Text segmentation	More difficult	Easier	No difference or no opinion
Less segmented hypertext	.12	.81	.06
More segmented hypertext	.09	.75	.16

Judgments of difficulty in locating information			
Text segmentation	Not obvious	Obvious	Mixed response
Less segmented hypertext	.22	.34	.44
More segmented hypertext	.0	.84	.16

response, indicating that it was easy to find the information for the solve task, but more difficult for the information location task. This is consistent with the design of the hypertexts and learning tasks.

Summary

The results of this research indicate that providing more structure in a hypertext facilitates the development of efficient and effective study strategies. Readers with the more segmented hypertext went directly to the most specific task-related units in studying the text, and were less likely to select irrelevant units than readers with the less segmented hypertext. These readers also became more efficient with experience in using the hypertext, decreasing the number of units selected with repeated use of the overview. Additionally, readers with the more segmented overview had no difficulty completing both learning tasks, whereas readers of the less segmented overview did not always locate the definitions for the information location task. Some readers gave up or selected poorer responses from other portions of the text. This difficulty in information location was reflected in readers' comments. Readers were overwhelmingly positive in their evaluations of both hypertexts, but readers of the less segmented hypertext noted that they had more difficulty finding the target content for the information location task. This suggests that when the text segmentation scheme obscures the location of task-relevant content, success in meeting the learning goal depends on whether the reader is sufficiently motivated to persist in text search.

As in the previously reported research, readers were better able to recall the title locations on the overview providing the most structure. Title location recall was better for the more segmented than the less segmented overview, for both the entire set of overview titles and for titles common to both overviews. This may again be due to the fact that the location of particular units is more distinct within a more variable spatial array. Additionally, recall of one title location within a branch could prompt recall of related titles with the more segmented overview.

Although title location memory was better for the more segmented overview, unit selection took longer with this overview than with the less segmented overview. This is in contrast to the previous research in which better title location recall coincided with shorter selection times. However, in the previous research, both overviews had the same number of titles, whereas the more segmented overview had more titles than the less segmented overview. It may be that the additional time needed to select from a larger set of units offsets the advantages in remembering title locations with the more segmented overview.

There were no differences in the amount of text content remembered with the two hypertexts. However, the recall of readers with the less segmented hypertext included a higher proportion of content from the segments of the text that did not contain target information (i.e., the second-level units of the more segmented hypertext). This is information that readers with the more segmented hypertext skipped (by selecting the most specific goal-related units and not selecting irrelevant units). In contrast, readers of the less segmented hypertext were required to skim through this content in searching for the target information, and also viewed more of this content through optional selection of irrelevant second-level units. Thus, the greater breadth of exposure to text content with the less segmented hypertext had a qualitative effect on recall in terms of what readers remembered, but it did not affect overall amount recalled.

DISCUSSION

The research summarized here examined the effects of providing structure in a hypertext overview on both readers' study strategies and the text representations developed for different learning goals. This was done by comparing structured hypertexts (i.e., hypertext with a hierarchically organized overview and a more segmented multilevel hypertext) with hypertexts having little structure (i.e., with a menu-like overview and a two-level structure consisting of relatively large units). The main findings are discussed next.

Overview Usability

Does the degree of structure provided in the overview influence readers' ability to develop efficient and effective study strategies for meeting their learning objective?

Providing structure in the overview enhanced hypertext usability in terms of the time spent selecting units (when the number of units to select from was constant), the ability to develop study strategies in the absence of a specific learning goal, and the ability to develop effective study strategies focusing on relevant content for a specific goal. Other research has similarly reported that readers work more efficiently when hypertext unit titles are organized as a map rather than a list (Monk, Walsh, & Dix, 1988). The results of the current research suggest that providing structure facilitates hypertext study by decreasing the time required for unit selection and by aiding readers in determining the information needed to meet their learning goals.

Unit Selection Times. Readers selected units more quickly from the hierarchical overview than from the list overview. This may have been related to differences in memory for title locations. Both the hierarchical overview and the more segmented overview facilitated recall of title locations relative to the less structured overviews to which they were compared. Memory for title locations may facilitate unit selection because readers do not have to search the overview, but could simply remember where the title was located. Memory for the more segmented overview did not decrease unit selection time, but this overview contained more titles than the less segmented overview.

The increased ability to recall title locations may be due in part to the greater variability in the spatial layout of the more structured overviews. Individual title locations were more distinct relative to the positions of other titles, so there were more cues for retrieving the title locations from memory. With the hierarchical overview, titles were organized into a two-dimensional tree structure as opposed to a list in which specific titles were either higher or lower relative to other titles; with the more segmented overview, titles were presented at three levels of a hierarchy with varying numbers of units at different levels as opposed to a two-level uniform circular array. Better unit location memory with the more structured overviews may also be related to the fact that the layouts were more meaningful because they indicated how the units were related. In this case, recall of the location of one unit may prompt recall for the location of related text units. Other researchers have similarly reported that spatial features of access facilities for computerized text databases can facilitate memory for how text units are related (Billingsley, 1982).

Study Strategies. The more structured overviews facilitated the development of effective study strategies focusing on content related to the learning goal. Compared to the less segmented hypertext, readers with the more segmented hypertext developed more efficient study strategies, skipping irrelevant units and selecting the most specific goal-related units. These readers also increased study efficiency with repeated experience using the overview. Similarly, in the absence of a specific learning goal, readers with the hierarchical overview were better able to develop review strategies and a well-integrated text representation compared to readers with the list overview. These results suggest that readers actively used the structure provided by the hypertext overviews to guide text study for a particular learning objective, or to develop a coherent representation of the text as a whole in the absence of a specific orienting goal. This is consistent with research on traditional text, indicating that skilled readers automatically attend to the topic structure of a text (i.e., the "macrostructure") even when it is not an explicit requirement of the study task (Guindon & Kintsch, 1984; Lorch, Lorch, & Matthews, 1985).

The effects of the less structured overviews on study strategies varied with the nature of the overview and the learning goal. With the list overview, readers tended to read the text once without reviewing. Readers who did review spent a relatively long time on the units they selected, suggesting that they were rereading entire units rather than strategically searching for specific content. The lack of review with this text suggests that in the absence of guidance from either the learning goal or structural information, readers were reluctant to expend the additional effort required to review. However, readers substantially increased their review of the list hypertext when given the summary goal, and consequently wrote summaries comparable to those written by readers of the structured texts. The increase in text review may have reflected readers' efforts to overcome the lack of organizational information by increasing their familiarity with the content through extra text processing. Research with traditional text has similarly found that readers' ability to structure poorly organized or unstructured text can vary according to the amount of additional text processing permitted (Kintsch, Mandel, & Kozminsky, 1977; Schwarz & Flammer, 1981). For example, Kintsch, Mandel, and Kozminsky (1977) found that readers wrote similar summaries of a story regardless of whether it was scrambled or organized, but they required more text study time prior to summarizing the scrambled story. The current research suggests that with the specific goal of writing a summary, readers were able to overcome processing difficulties posed by the lack of structure in the list overview with repeated text review.

In contrast to the list hypertext, readers with the less segmented hypertext had difficulty using this overview successfully even with specific learning objectives. Readers were more likely to select irrelevant units from this overview, and tended to give up or select poorer answers when the location of the task-related content was not readily apparent. Although research with traditional text indicates that readers can often successfully use poorly or inappropriately organized text (Dee-Lucas & Larkin, 1990; Eylon & Reif, 1984), the ability to do this varies with the skill level of the reader and the structural characteristics of the text (Kintsch, 1990; Kintsch, Mandel, & Kozminsky, 1977). For example, Kintsch, Mandel, and Kozminsky (1977) found that the ability to summarize scrambled stories depended on how well the content could be matched to a familiar story structure. The results of the current research suggest that success with less structured overviews depends on the degree to which the lack of structure hinders readers' ability to identify goal-related content. If the processing difficulty is extensive, then the degree to which readers are motivated to persist in text study may determine whether they achieve their objective. Research on different types of hypertext navigation systems has similarly shown that their effectiveness varies with the extent to which they reduce the processing load required to achieve the study goal (Wright & Lickorish, 1990; see also Stanton, Taylor, & Tweedie, 1992).

Text Representations

Does the overview structure affect qualitative and quantitative characteristics of the resulting text representation?

The results of this research indicate that differently structured overviews direct readers' attention to different aspects of the text, resulting in qualitative but not quantitative differences in the text representations. Although there were differences between hypertexts in the amount of text review, the nature of the study strategies, and the breadth of text content skimmed or explored, there were no differences in overall amount recalled or number of units remembered. There were, however, qualitative differences in the degree of unit integration and the content of the text representations.

Readers with the list overview had difficulty adequately summarizing the main points of the text after studying with the general learning goal. In order to identify the main points of a text, readers must integrate the content into a unified representation so they can determine the central ideas within the context of the entire text. The results of this research suggest that readers with an overview lacking organizational information do not necessarily integrate hypertext units in this way unless required to do so. Research with traditional text has similarly shown that readers can have difficulty determining the main ideas if the text is poorly structured or lacks structure (Dee-Lucas & Larkin, 1990; Kieras, 1980; Kintsch & Yarbrough, 1982). Kintsch and Yarbrough (1982) found that readers had more difficulty answering questions about the text topic and main ideas when studying texts with randomly ordered paragraphs (excluding organizational cues), as opposed to well-structured versions of the same content. They note that readers in this study would most likely have been able to organize the scrambled texts and determine the main points if they had been motivated to devote additional effort to the task. The results of the current research similarly indicate that in the absence of a learning objective encouraging readers to organize the text, readers with unstructured hypertext may not expend the effort required to integrate the text units into a unified representation. This is consistent with other research indicating that hypertext formats can hinder the acquisition of main ideas (Gordon, Gustavel, Moore, & Hankey, 1988).

In contrast, readers with the hierarchical overview wrote summaries comparable to readers of the traditional control text, regardless of the nature of the learning goal. Thus, readers used the structural information provided on the overview even when it was not demanded by the learning goal. As noted earlier, readers with traditional text have also been found to attend to organizational characteristics of text as an integral part of text comprehension (Guindon &

Kintsch, 1984; Lorch, Lorch, & Matthews, 1985). However, traditional text contains structural information within the body of the text itself, which is encountered automatically in the process of reading. In the case of hypertext, this organizational information is presented external to the text content so that readers must integrate the structural information from the overview with the content of the units. The results of the current research suggest that readers of hypertext use this structural information even though it is distinct from the text content. This may be due in part to the emphasis given to the structural information when it is presented on the overview. Providing an explicit content structure on the hypertext overview may encourage readers to think about the unit interrelationships, as well as indicate the text organization (Salomon, 1988). This finding is consistent with research by Lorch and Lorch (1985) on structural overviews for traditional text (i.e., introductory paragraphs presenting the text topics and their organization). They found that readers given scrambled texts used the information in structural overviews to develop a coherent topic representation (a representation of the main topics and their interrelationships), as indicated by the number of topics included in recall. The structural information provided in hypertext overviews is similarly used by readers to interrelate the text units into a unified representation of all or a portion of the hypertext.

There were also qualitative differences in the representations for the more or less segmented hypertexts which more directly reflected differences in text study strategies. Recall for the less segmented hypertext contained proportionally more content from second-level units (as defined by the more segmented overview). This reflects the fact that readers with the less segmented overview selected more irrelevant second-level units and skimmed through second-level content at the beginning of the larger units for this hypertext. In contrast, readers with the more segmented hypertext selected the most specific goal-relevant units (third-level units). Thus, there was a trade-off in learning efficiency and breadth of recall, with the more focused text study for the more segmented hypertext resulting in recall of a narrower range of content.

However, readers with the less segmented hypertext did not recall more information overall than readers with the more segmented hypertext. Thus, the increase in recall of second-level content with this hypertext was accompanied by a decrease in recall of third-level content. This suggests that readers with the less segmented hypertext were more selective in processing the third-level unit content than readers with the more segmented hypertext. Research with traditional text has generally shown that readers focus on the text information relevant to their goal (Anderson, 1982). For example, readers spend longer on sentences containing task-relevant information (Lorch, Lorch, & Mogan, 1987) and recall different types of information when studying a text for different purposes (Schmalhofer & Glavanov, 1986). The current research suggests that the nature of selective processing with hypertext varies with unit size as well as with the relevance of the content. The text recalls suggest that the larger units of the less segmented hypertext resulted in more selective processing of the task-related segments of the units than did the smaller units of the more segmented hypertext. Readers of the less segmented hypertext may have used the second-level content at the beginning of the larger combined units to guide processing of the subsequent third-level content. It may also be the case that because the units were larger and presented as one continuous text segment, readers distributed their attention more evenly over the unit as a whole, resulting in more recall of second-level units and less of third-level units compared to readers with the more segmented text (who focused on the content of the third-level units). Conversely, readers with the more segmented hypertext may have been less selective in processing the third-level units because these units were relatively small, and could easily be processed as a whole.

Although there were no quantitative differences in recall of the more and less structured hypertexts, it is possible that such effects would be found with larger hypertexts. For example, in the current research there was no difference in amount recalled from the list and hierarchical hypertexts with the general learning goal, even though readers with the list hypertext had not integrated the text units into a coherent representation (as indicated by their summaries). However, in the case of a hypertext having a larger number of units, the lack of a coherent topic representation may result in recall of fewer topics (i.e., the topics that were not integrated into a representation of the text topic structure would be forgotten). This would result in less overall recall because some topics would not be available as recall prompts for their related unit content (Lorch & Lorch, 1985). In the case of the more and less segmented hypertexts, the trade-off in efficiency and breadth of exposure to text content found in the current research could affect overall recall if the difference in the amount of content read with the two hypertexts was large. If readers with the more segmented hypertext selected many fewer units, or if these units were much smaller than those in the less segmented hypertext, then the difference in the amount of text content viewed could be great enough to produce quantitative differences in text recall, in addition to differences in the distribution of attention over units. This would be influenced by the nature of the learning task, in addition to the size and structure of the hypertext.

Reader Evaluations

Does the degree of structure provided by the overview affect readers' judgments of the usability of the hypertext?

Readers generally preferred the type of hypertext used in this research to traditional printed text, even when the overview was somewhat difficult to use. Regardless of the overview structure, most readers judged their experimental hypertext as easier to use than printed text. All readers in all experiments indicated that the main advantage of the hypertexts was the easy access to information provided by the overviews. Additionally, readers with the hierarchical overview stated that the hypertext aided them in determining the organization of the content.

Readers of the list hypertext also indicated this as an advantage when they had the summary goal, even though this overview did not provide structural information. This suggests that for some learning goals, simply providing a preview of text topics may give readers a better sense of how to achieve the goal. In contrast, list hypertext readers with the general learning goal indicated that they had difficulty organizing the text content. These contrasting evaluations of the list hypertext show that readers' perceptions of the usability of hypertext reflects the ease with which they can meet their learning goals (Edwards & Hardman, 1989). Other research has shown that readers prefer different types of navigation systems for different tasks and text organizations with hypertext (Allinson & Hammond, 1989; Wright & Lickorish, 1990). However, readers in the current research strongly preferred the hypertexts to traditional printed text, even when the overview structure hindered task completion, as was the case with the less segmented hypertext. It may be that the direct access to information provided by the hypertexts gave readers a greater sense of control over the learning material. Because this was a particularly salient feature, it may have resulted in the overall positive evaluations of the hypertexts (Becker & Dwyer, 1994; Gay, Trumbull, & Smith, 1988; Small & Grabowski, 1992).

CONCLUSIONS

The results of this research indicate that providing structure for hypertext units on an overview has both advantages and disadvantages. At a general level, the findings indicate that readers attend to the structural information, using it both in developing a representation for the text content, and in generating efficient and effective study strategies. To the extent that the structure increases the meaningfulness and distinctiveness of the overview layout, providing structure also enhances memory for the title locations and facilitates unit selection.

On the other hand, because structure increases study efficiency, readers are less likely to encounter related nontarget content when using highly structured overviews. There may be less exploration of the hypertext, and readers may go directly to the most specific goal-related unit, rather than following pathways to that node. Thus, the greater efficiency with more structured overviews can result in less breadth of learning by reducing the range of text content read. This suggests that different types of overview structure may be appropriate for different types of study objectives (e.g., general browsing vs. looking up factual information; Allinson & Hammond, 1989; Wright & Lickorish, 1990).

Although this research found that providing structure offers several advantages, in some circumstances, less structured overviews may be more appropriate. Less structured hypertexts can accommodate a variety of learning goals and individual differences by allowing readers to organize the content according to their own goals and learning preferences. If readers are able to structure the content successfully, these reader-generated structures may better meet the readers' needs. In the current research, readers with less structured overviews were able to use them effectively when they had a specific learning objective (providing a task around which to organize the information) and when they were sufficiently motivated to persist in text search (when the lack of structure hampered information location). These results suggest that the effective use of less structured overviews may depend more heavily on reader characteristics such as general learning skills, motivation, and subject matter expertise.

This research compared hypertext study strategies and representations developed with overviews that were appropriately structured or less structured. It did not examine the effect of inappropriate structure in the hypertext overview. In situations where readers have to restructure an existing organization, the effects of structured overviews may differ. Research with traditional text suggests that when readers successfully reorganize existing text structures, they can develop a deeper understanding of the content due to more thorough processing of the text content (Kintsch, 1990; Mannes & Kintsch, 1987). In the current research, there was no evidence that the processing difficulties associated with the less structured overviews resulted in a deeper comprehension of the content. However, this research focused on measures of recall rather than on indicators of depth of understanding, such as information application. Such effects may be apparent with different dependent measures from those used in this research.

ACKNOWLEDGMENTS

This research was supported by National Science Foundation Grant No. MDR-8855631 and a grant from The Spencer Foundation awarded to Diana Dee-Lucas and Jill H. Larkin. The research was conducted in collaboration with Jill Larkin. The data presented, the statements made, and the views expressed are solely the responsibility of the author. Portions of this chapter were presented in a poster session at the Hypertext '91 ACM Conference on Hypertext, San Antonio, Texas, December 1991, and at the ED-MEDIA '95 World Conference on Educational Multimedia and Hypermedia, Graz, Austria, June 1995. The author thanks Jill Larkin for her comments on the chapter, and Dan Adler for his help in data collection and analysis in this research.

REFERENCES

Allinson, L., & Hammond, N. (1989). A learning support environment: The hitch-hiker's guide. In R. McAleese (Ed.), *Hypertext: Theory and practice* (pp. 62–74). Oxford, England: Intellect Books.

Anderson, R. C. (1982). Allocation of attention during reading. In A. Flammer & W. Kintsch (Eds.), *Discourse processing* (pp. 292–305). Amsterdam: North-Holland Publishing Co.

Becker, D. A., & Dwyer, M. M. (1994). Using hypermedia to provide learner control. *Journal of Educational Multimedia and Hypermedia, 3,* 155–172.

Bergeron, B. (1994). Personalized data representation: Supporting the individual needs of knowledge workers. *Journal of Educational Multimedia and Hypermedia, 3,* 93–109.

Billingsley, P. A. (1982). Navigation through hierarchical menu structures: Does it help to have a map? *Proceedings of the Human Factors Society, 26th Annual Meeting* (pp. 103–107). Santa Monica, CA: Human Factors Society.

Brooks, L. W., & Dansereau, D. F. (1983). Effects of structural schema training and text organization on expository prose processing. *Journal of Educational Psychology, 75,* 811–820.

Charney, D. (1987). Comprehending non-linear text: The role of discourse cues and reading strategies. *Proceedings of Hypertext '87* (pp. 109–120). New York: Association for Computing Machinery.

Dee-Lucas, D., & Larkin, J. H. (1990). Organization and comprehensibility in scientific proofs, or "Consider a particle p. . . ." *Journal of Educational Psychology, 82,* 701–714.

Dee-Lucas, D., & Larkin, J. H. (1995). Learning from electronic texts: Effects of interactive overviews for information access. *Cognition and Instruction, 13,* 431–468.

Edwards, D. M., & Hardman, L. (1989). Lost in hyperspace: Cognitive mapping and navigation in a hypertext environment. In R. McAleese (Ed.), *Hypertext: Theory and practice* (pp. 105–125). Oxford, England: Intellect Books.

Eylon, B., & Reif, F. (1984). Effects of knowledge organization on task performance. *Cognition and Instruction, 1,* 5–44.

Gay, G., Trumbull, D., & Smith, J. (1988). Perceptions of control and use of control options in computer-assisted video instruction. *TechTrends, 33,* 31–33.

Gordon, S., Gustavel, J., Moore, J., & Hankey, J. (1988). The effect of hypertext on reader knowledge representation. In *Proceedings of the 32nd Annual Meeting of the Human Factors Society* (pp. 296–300). Santa Monica: Human Factors Society.

Guindon, R., & Kintsch, W. (1984). Priming macropropositions: Evidence for the primacy of macropropositions in the memory for text. *Journal of Verbal Learning and Verbal Behavior, 23,* 508–518.

Halasz, F., & Conklin, J. (1989). *Issues in the design and application of hypermedia systems.* Tutorial No. 26 presented at the CHI '89 Conference on Computer Human Interaction, Austin, TX.

Heller, R. S. (1990). The role of hypermedia in education: A look at the research issues. *Journal of Research in Computing in Education, 22,* 431–441.

Jonassen, D. H. (1986). Hypertext principles for text and courseware design. *Educational Psychologist, 21,* 269–292.

Kieras, D. E. (1980). Initial mention as a signal to thematic content in technical passages. *Memory & Cognition, 8,* 345–353.

Kintsch, E. (1990). Macroprocesses and microprocesses in the development of summarization skill. *Cognition and Instruction, 7,* 161–195.

Kintsch, W. (1986). Learning from text. *Cognition and Instruction, 3,* 87–108.

Kintsch, W., Mandel, T. S., & Kozminsky, E. (1977). Summarizing scrambled stories. *Memory & Cognition, 5,* 547–552.

Kintsch, W., & Yarbrough, J. C. (1982). The role of rhetorical structure in text comprehension. *Journal of Educational Psychology, 74,* 828–834.

Lorch, R. F., Jr., & Lorch, E. P. (1985). Topic structure representation and text recall. *Journal of Educational Psychology, 77,* 137–148.

Lorch, R. F., Jr., Lorch, E. P., & Matthews, P. D. (1985). On-line processing of the topic structure of a text. *Discourse Processes, 10,* 63–80.

Lorch, R. F., Jr., Lorch, E. P., & Mogan, A. M. (1987). Task effects and individual differences in on-line processing of the topic structure of a text. *Discourse Processes, 10,* 63–80.

Mannes, S. M., & Kintsch, W. (1987). The role of knowledge in discourse comprehension: A construction-integration model. *Cognition and Instruction, 4,* 91–115.

Mayes, T., Kibby, M. R., & Anderson, A. (1990). Signposts for conceptual orientation: Some requirements for learning from hypertext. In R. McAleese & C. Green (Eds.), *Hypertext: State of the art* (pp. 121–129). Oxford: Intellect.

Monk, A. F., Walsh, P., & Dix, A. J. (1988). A comparison of hypertext, scrolling, and folding as mechanisms for program browsing. In D. M. Jones & R. Winer (Eds.), *People and computers IV: Proceedings of the 4th conference of the British Computer Society* (pp. 421–435). Cambridge, England: Cambridge University Press.

Salomon, G. (1988). AI in reverse: Computer tools that turn cognitive. *Journal of Educational Computing Research, 4,* 123–139.

Schmalhofer, F., & Glavanov, D. (1986). Three components of understanding a programmer's manual: Verbatim, propositional, and situational representations. *Journal of Memory and Language, 25,* 279–294.

Schwarz, M. N. K., & Flammer, A. (1981). Text structure and title—Effects on comprehension and recall. *Journal of Verbal Learning and Verbal Behavior, 20,* 61–66.

Small, R. V., & Grabowski, B. L. (1992). An exploratory study of information-seeking behaviors and learning with hypermedia information systems. *Journal of Educational Multimedia and Hypermedia, 1,* 445–464.

Stanton, N. A., Taylor, R. G., & Tweedie, L. A. (1992). Maps as navigational aids in hypertext environments: An empirical evaluation. *Journal of Educational Multimedia and Hypermedia, 1,* 431–444.

Tsai, C. (1988). Hypertext: Technology, applications, and research issues. *Journal of Educational Technology Systems, 17,* 3–14.

van Dijk, T., & Kintsch, W. (1983). *Strategies of discourse comprehension.* New York: Academic Press.

Weyer, S. A. (1982). The design of a dynamic book for information search. *International Journal of Man-Machine Studies, 17,* 87–107.

Wright, P., & Lickorish, A. (1990). An empirical comparison of two navigation systems for two hypertexts. In R. McAleese & C. Green (Eds.), *Hypertext: State of the art* (pp. 84–93). Oxford, England: Intellect Books.

6

▼▼▼▼▼▼▼

Comprehension, Coherence, and Strategies in Hypertext and Linear Text

Peter W. Foltz
New Mexico State University

Hypertext presents a new way to read online text that differs from reading standard linear text. Text is typically presented in a linear form, in which there is a single way to progress through the text, starting at the beginning and reading to the end. However, in hypertext, information can be represented in a semantic network where multiple related sections of the text are connected to each other. A user may then browse through the sections of the text, jumping from one text section to another. This permits a reader to choose the path through the text that is most relevant to his or her interests.

The features in hypertext supply flexibility to the reader when compared to reading linear text such as books. Clearly, some of this flexibility does exist in books (e.g., table of contents and indices), but it is not as widely used or exploited. Hypertext permits readers to use these features automatically rather than requiring readers to manually refer to them as needed. This provides additional control to the reader in determining the order in which the text is to be read, and allows the reader to read the text as if it were specifically tailored to the reader's background and interests. This flexibility does promise an advantage of person-alization and eases the burden of finding information. However, is this flexibility actually good or useful to the reader?

The concept of using the associative paths in hypertext to retrieve and read information has caused great excitement. The promise of universally available hypertexts has been touted as "a seamless and reunited computer world" (adver-tisement for the Xanadu Hypertext), having "the potential to become a significant application area; equalling or perhaps exceeding that of word processing, spreadsheets and general database applications" (Begoray, 1990, p. 121), and "because hypertext has the power to change the way we understand and experience texts, it offers radical promises and challenges to students, teachers and theorists of literature" (Landow, 1989, p. 174). Using associative retrieval paths is similar to the way retrieval is performed from human memory, and this may be part of the appeal of hypertext to researchers and developers when they state that hypertext systems will improve a user's ability to find and use information.

Although a variety of hypertexts have been developed over the past 20 years, it is often not clear whether there are strong advantages for hypertext. Research in hypertext has often failed to show any significant advantages for reading a hypertext compared to the equivalent text in linear form. In addition, the effectiveness of the various features that can be used in hypertexts can vary greatly depending on the domain and content of the text and the goals of the reader. Up to this point, no standards or definitive rules exist on how to develop an effective hypertext. However, because hypertext encompasses such domains as user–interface design, psychology, education, and information retrieval, theory from these domains can be applied to hypertext in order to aid in the understanding and development of effective hypertexts.

The last 40 years has seen the development of a large body of research that focuses on linear text comprehension, both from a theoretical and an evaluative standpoint. Text research has permitted predictions of comprehension based on such factors as the structure of the text, the background knowledge of the reader, and the reader's abilities. This chapter examines the evaluation of hypertext from the perspective of text comprehension.

APPROACHES TO DEVELOPING HYPERTEXT

Research in Hypertext

The development of hypertext systems has created research into how to design and use hypertexts. Much of this research has focused on computer science and interface issues rather than on the cognitive aspects of hypertexts. Some of the major areas of hypertext research include the development of the underlying representations of information and connections (e.g., Botafogo & Shneiderman, 1991; Furuta & Stotts, 1989), methods of connecting, structuring, and retrieving the information (e.g., Croft & Turtle, 1989; Crouch, Crouch, & Andreas, 1989), designing hypertexts for supporting argumentation (e.g., Conklin & Begeman, 1989; Fischer, McCall, & Morch, 1989), studying information seeking in hypertexts (e.g., Marchionini & Shneiderman, 1987; Weyer, 1982), and the role of rhetoric and writing in hypertexts (e.g., Bolter, 1991; Britton & Glynn, 1989).

Although there have been a variety of areas of research on hypertext, one of the primary goals of the research has been to evaluate hypertexts and hypertext features in order to bring about improvements. From this research, we can then get an idea as to how well hypertexts have succeeded and what hypertext features are the most effective.

Evaluation of Hypertexts. Research comparing hypertext to linear text provides some measure as to what situations will be best suited for the presentation of textual information using hypertext. There have been claims of the superiority of hypertext over linear text (e.g., Martin, 1990; Nelson, 1967), however, research into this area has not been uniformly successful in showing an advantage for hypertext. The chapter by Rouet and Levonen (in this volume) discusses the details of these studies. Overall, the results of the studies vary greatly. A large part of the variability may be due to the different tasks, hypertext systems, subjects, and the types of texts used. Therefore, the results indicate that there are several factors that must be considered in order to determine whether a hypertext or a linear text would work best.

Because hypertexts have incorporated many new features that are not found in linear text, such as linking, the ability to search for information, guided tours, and overview maps, it is often unclear which of the features may be effective in improving the users' ability to read and comprehend the text. Without information about what features work best, it is difficult to know what features to incorporate into the design of a new hypertext. For this reason, there have been studies comparing the various hypertext features.

One factor that may affect reading hypertext is the resolution of the screen. Work by Gould (Gould & Grischkowsky, 1984; Gould et al., 1987) found that reading time was significantly slower when reading a text on a computer screen as compared to reading the same text on paper. However, when a high resolution screen with antialiased fonts was used, the reading speeds were equivalent. Thus, studies comparing linear text on paper to hypertexts on screens may find some reading differences due merely to the resolution of the text rather than to any factors of the actual structure of the text. For this reason, research that compares hypertext and linear texts should ensure that they both have equivalent resolution of the text.

With the multiple paths that are possible when reading a hypertext, there is a greater navigation load on the reader than with linear text. In order to simplify the reader's task then, additional navigation features must be provided. In a linear text, a table of contents and an index are the two typical navigational features. Because linear text is often organized hierarchically, the table of contents serves as an outline with pointers to pages for each entry. However, in a hypertext, the structure may be much more complicated. For that reason, a common feature in a hypertext is a map. A map permits a reader to see a representation of the text's structure along with the relationships between the different text sections. Monk, Walsh, and Dix (1988) found that with a map, subjects were much faster at being able to answer questions in a hypertext than with no map. However, in a similar study, Hammond and Allinson (1989) found no differences in answer accuracy or task time whether or not a map was provided. Nevertheless, they found that with a map, subjects did tend to visit more of the text nodes than the subjects who did not have a map. There were large differences in the style of navigation based on the subject's task. Subjects who were instructed to just explore the information space tended to use a guided tour facility, whereas subjects with the more directed tasks of answering particular questions used mostly the map and index to help navigate.

Thus, we see that there are varying results as to whether certain features aid the user of a hypertext. In addition, factors such as the user's goals and background knowledge can influence whether a particular feature is useful. Nielsen (1989) performed a meta-analysis of 92 benchmark measures that had been taken from usability issues tested in hypertext research. In all of the measures he examined, he found that there were actually very few results that had large effects. From this analysis, he concluded that there are actually very few studies that have shown the real world impact of hypertext systems. In addition, the lack of strong effects in this area of research could mostly be explained by large individual differences among users, tasks, and texts. Thus, although there has been a lot of research in hypertext, few concrete results exist to provide strong evidence on how well hypertexts will work or guidelines on how to create effective hypertexts.

Guidelines for Developing Hypertexts

Another source of how to develop hypertexts comes from development guidelines. Several books and articles have been published containing guidelines and rules for hypertext development (Martin, 1990; Nielsen, 1990). These guidelines concentrate on issues such as how much text should be contained in a node, what hypertext features to use, and how the information should be structured. However, most of these guidelines do not provide concrete design rules based on theory, but instead present abstract rules based more on common sense.[1] The fact that the rules are fairly abstract is not surprising given that writing a hypertext is as difficult, if not more difficult, than writing linear text. With linear text, we do have some guidelines, but they still are somewhat abstract, and effective writing depends more on large amounts of practice than on just being able to follow a set of writing rules. In addition, the style of writing will depend greatly on the points the author wants to express and the domain in which the author is writing.

Theory-Based Approaches to Hypertext Design and Evaluation

The studies described earlier shed some light on what features may be used to develop a good hypertext system, however, they are very insular, only examining particular features with particular texts. Without an ability to generalize outside

---

[1]"For the short term, the best recommendation probably is to pay close attention to the authoring principles implicit in other writers' hypertexts and try to emulate the principles you like" (Nielsen, 1990, p. 164).

of the texts and tasks, with every new feature or text developed, another evaluation study would need to be performed to determine its effectiveness. An alternative approach is to use a theoretical background to drive the design of the hypertext. This then would permit comparisons of features by using the theory to make the performance predictions. Theory-based approaches have been used in the study of human–computer interactions (e.g., Card, Moran, & Newell, 1983; Kieras & Polson, 1985; Lewis & Polson, 1990). These approaches use a theoretical model of the user and system in order to derive predictions of usability. They typically involve modeling such factors as the users' knowledge, possible states of the computer, and possible actions a user can take, and have had some success at predicting usability of systems and of particular features. Although theory-based design has not been fully incorporated into the majority of software designers, its success for designing interfaces suggests that it can similarly be used for the design of hypertext systems.

There have been a few theoretical approaches to studying and designing hypertext. Although these approaches were not based on some of the strict modeling criteria used in the modeling mentioned above, these approaches did use theoretical bases or guidelines for their development and testing. One approach has been to use user–interface guidelines, such as dialog rules, to determine how a hypertext interface should be designed (Hardman & Sharrat, 1989; Shneiderman, 1987). This approach permits pieces of the interface of a hypertext to be developed based on proven guidelines. A second approach has been to use "formative design evaluation" (Egan et al., 1989; Landauer et al., 1993). In formative design evaluation, development and changes of features are based on psychological guidelines. Behavioral studies are then performed on the system in order to determine what features can be improved and in what ways. This iterative design method allows a comparison of the features and quantitative measures of the improvements from previous versions. A third approach has been to develop hypertexts from the point of view of information retrieval theory. In this approach, models from information retrieval have been applied in order to determine how to structure the information. These methods include probabilistic models of retrieval (Croft & Turtle, 1989), hierarchical clustering (Crouch et al., 1989), and petri nets (Furuta & Stotts, 1989) in order to connect the nodes of information. A more cognitively based approach is the cognitive flexibility theory (Spiro & Jehng, 1990). Cognitive flexibility theory represents the textual information in multiple perspectives that permit the reader to learn and use the information flexibly.

Although these approaches have helped improve the design of hypertexts, one area that has been neglected is the consideration of the text in terms of its discourse cues. Charney (1987, 1994) suggested this area as a possible area for improving hypertexts. However, thus far, there has been little theoretical research in this area. This may be partially due to the fact that up to this point, developers of hypertexts tend to be primarily computer scientists and not psychologists with the skills and background in issues of text comprehension. Thus, a different theoretical approach to hypertext is to examine it in terms of text comprehension and discourse cues.

TEXT COMPREHENSION RESEARCH
AND HYPERTEXT

Over the past 30 years, there has been a large amount of research in text comprehension, primarily in the fields of psychology and education. The goals of text comprehension research are to understand what factors in the reader and in the text influence the ease of comprehending a text and to make some predictions as to how easy a text will be to comprehend. Through modeling both the text and the reader's knowledge and abilities, researchers have been able to develop both better texts and a better understanding of the human comprehension processes.

Research in text comprehension has examined a variety of factors that influence comprehension. These factors include the role of coherence in a text, the role of the readers' background knowledge, the role of the narrative schema of the text, and the role of the reader's cognitive abilities. In addition, studies have examined the strategies readers use when going through a text and the role these strategies can play for comprehending a text. Not only do these factors play a major role in linear text comprehension, they also play an equally important role in the comprehending of hypertexts.

Predictions of Comprehension

Modeling Comprehension.   Hypertext differs from linear text in some fundamental ways. A hypertext provides more flexibility to the reader in choosing where to go in the text. A hypertext also provides the reader with more methods to employ in order to find the relevant information in the text and to move through the different sections of the text. However, aside from these differences, the primary goal of both hypertexts and linear texts is to convey information in a coherent form to a reader. In this manner, the reader should be able to extract the relevant information from the text that reflects the intended goals of both the author and the reader. For this reason, we can examine the implications of the results from research in text comprehension in the design and evaluation of hypertexts.

Researchers in the field of text comprehension have used user models to predict what information will be learned from a linear text. One primary approach has been to examine comprehension using the Kintsch model of text comprehension (Kintsch, 1988; van Dijk & Kintsch, 1983). The Kintsch model has been used for predicting the comprehension of text based on such factors as what features will be remembered from the text (van Dijk & Kintsch, 1983), the role of background knowledge (Britton & Gulgoz, 1991; van Dijk & Kintsch, 1983), the role of coherence and readability (Kintsch & Vipond, 1979), and also goal planning in such domains as computer mail systems (Mannes & Kintsch, 1991) and the UNIX operating system (Doane, Kintsch, & Polson, 1989).

When reading a linear text, processing occurs at many levels. These levels range from the low level processes of recognizing individual words up to high level processes of deriving the gist of the information in the text. These processes work together simultaneously to extract meaning from the text. Meaning, however, is represented at different levels. In the Kintsch model, the reader's memory for text is represented at three levels; a surface representation of the words and sentences, the meaning of the text (textbase), and a general representation of what is described by the text incorporating outside background knowledge (situation model). As text is read, the text is incorporated into the readers' representation of the information. Information from the surface representation of the text is quickly lost (e.g., Bransford & Franks, 1971). However, some of the abstracted information from the surface structure of the text is incorporated into the textbase, represented as propositions. Propositions serve as semantic primitives representing the information acquired (e.g., Fodor, Fodor, & Garrett, 1975; Kintsch, 1974).

The propositions are connected to each other in the textbase through semantic coherence relations. In semantic coherence, constituents of the text will be coherent if they share some form of semantic relatedness in the discourse. The amount of coherence is therefore represented by the amount of shared meaning and referential relations. These coherence relations are based on standard rhetorical devices in the text, such as causality, use of pronouns, and word repetition. The semantic coherence can be represented both at the local level of individual propositions in the textbase and at the global level of the macrostructure of the text.

The mental representation of these interconnected propositions in the textbase (coherence graph) takes the form of a hierarchical structure with higher level concepts represented as superordinate propositions that are connected to lower level concepts represented as subordinate propositions (Kintsch & van Dijk, 1978). Recall of propositions follows this hierarchy, with propositions from the upper part of the tree being more likely to be recalled than lower level propositions (Britton, Meyer, Hodge, & Glynn, 1980; Kintsch & Keenan, 1973; Meyer, 1973). At a higher level, readers generate a macrostructure or gist of the text. The macrostructure is the result of the readers' inferential processes, with readers forming hypotheses of the overall meaning of paragraphs, chapters, and whole books. In this manner, the macrostructure incorporates the reader's background knowledge with the text in forming these hypotheses. The resulting macrostructure of the text is similar to the textbase in that it is also represented as a hierarchical structure with higher level concepts represented at the top.

The Role of Coherence.   The process of incorporating propositions into the textbase is a process of maintaining coherence. Propositions that have overlapping arguments, and thus are semantically related, create coherence. However, if the current proposition being processed does not share arguments with propositions in short term memory, then a bridging inference must be made by the reader in order to maintain coherence (e.g., Kintsch & van Dijk, 1978). When a reader makes a bridging inference, the reader must use knowledge from his or her situation model in order to fill in the missing information. Writers often assume readers will have the appropriate background knowledge to make the proper bridging inferences, and therefore, that knowledgeable readers will make these inferences automatically. However, if a reader does not have the proper background knowledge, these inferences consume additional resources of the reader, typically resulting in lower comprehension. Thus, the amount of coherence in the text can be used to make predictions of comprehension (e.g., Kintsch & Vipond, 1979; Miller & Kintsch, 1980). Coherence of a text can be assessed by converting a text into its propositions and then calculating the number of arguments that overlap from one proposition to the next. A greater amount of propositional overlap corresponds to a greater amount of coherence.

One application of this predictive power has been to improve the comprehensibility of texts. Britton and Gulgoz (1991) used the Kintsch model to identify locations in a text where a reader would have to make these bridging inferences in order to maintain coherence of the text. The chosen text was on the topic of the air war in Vietnam and so undergraduates had very little background knowledge to make the correct bridging inferences at these incoherent locations. They created a revised version of the text in which they inserted into the text the inferences that needed to be made at the various locations. They found that undergraduates reading the revised text had significantly better recall and a better mental representation of the text than those who had read the original version.

In a linear text, a writer typically maintains a set of coherent arguments through the text. At the local level, a writer makes words and sentences flow together through common referents. At a global level, a writer similarly makes paragraphs and sections flow from one to the other in a coherent manner. This aids the reader in structuring the information in the text to fit into the knowledge structures of what has been read previously. If there is little global coherence between sections, then the user must make bridging inferences in order to maintain coherence (e.g., Kintsch & Vipond, 1979). For readers without appropriate background knowledge, these inferences can consume the resources of the reader, typically resulting in lower comprehension.

In a hypertext, at any text section there are usually a variety of other sections to which a reader can jump. However, it may not be possible for a writer to anticipate all the possible places to which a reader may jump and therefore, it may also not be possible to maintain good macrocoherence for all possible links. Although the writer of the hypertext may code all the links, it would still be difficult to write each section so that it would cohere well with every possible section to which a reader could jump. Jumps which are not coherent could result in an additional processing load for the reader, as the reader generates the necessary inferences to incorporate the textual information from the new node into what has been previously read. Thus, many of the possible links in a hypertext may cause difficulty in the reader's comprehension.

One exception to this problem of hypertext coherence may be found in argument-based hypertext systems (e.g., Conklin & Begeman, 1989; Fischer et al., 1989). These systems take into account the role of coherence by only allowing jumps between nodes where a coherent argument has been previously set. These coherent links are created through careful hand coding of all possible links. Although argument-based hypertext involves a lot more hand crafting in order to create only these coherent links, it avoids the problems of readers jumping to nodes using links that may cause an incoherent transition.

The Role of Background Knowledge.   As a text is read, there is a large cognitive load on the reader as the reader is decoding the text and incorporating the textual information into his or her knowledge base. The key to incorporating the information into the reader's knowledge base is partly dependent on the amount of background knowledge of the reader. A reader's background knowledge permits the information to be incorporated into preexisting knowledge structures. So, readers who do not have an adequate amount of background knowledge on the subject of a text will have a lower comprehension of the text (Spilich, Vesonder, Chiesi, & Voss, 1979; Voss, Vesonder, & Spilich, 1980). The background knowledge enables the reader to provide a coherence to the text, permitting better bridging inferences between noncoherent sections and also permitting additional elaborative inferences. In addition, there is evidence that the background knowledge influences the processing of information at the situational model level, but not at the propositional level (Fincher-Kiefer, Post, Greene, & Voss, 1988). Thus, additional background knowledge of the text makes it easier for developing relevant macropropositions, resulting in a better representation of the text for the reader.

The amount of background knowledge can also differentially affect the readers of a hypertext. As in linear text, readers with background knowledge on the domain of the text will be better at encoding information from the text than those without the background knowledge. The high knowledge readers will have the correct conceptual structures in which to integrate the new information and therefore, the reader will tend to have better recall of the text.

However, due to the flexibility of hypertexts, readers with little background knowledge may have additional difficulties when compared to readers of equivalent linear texts. Readers with background knowledge will already have the correct conceptual structures for the domain. The hypertext structure may therefore be very familiar for them. However, a reader with little knowledge of the domain of the text will not be familiar with the structure of the hypertext. Because one of the concepts of hypertext is to permit the reader more flexibility in choosing where to go, a low knowledge reader may not be able to accurately choose the relevant text sections. Thus, low knowledge readers may have additional problems of navigating through the hypertext structure. This problem may not be as evident in linear texts, because the linear text provides a single (default) path to read through the text. Low knowledge readers can always take this path, even if they are having trouble comprehending the text.

The Role of Narrative Schema.   Similar to the background knowledge, the narrative schema of a text can aid in the comprehension of that text. A knowledgeable reader can use the narrative schema to provide a structure with which to organize the text (e.g., Black & Bower, 1979; Dillon, 1991; van Dijk & Kintsch, 1983). Placing a text in a well-known narrative schema can improve the comprehension of that text (e.g., Poulsen, Kintsch, Kintsch, & Premack, 1979).

In linear texts, there are a variety of common narrative schemata employed. Most readers are familiar with them and can use their knowledge of a schema in order to help structure and integrate the textual information. However, a narrative schema is primarily dependent on a familiar organization of the presentation of the information. With the novel structures found in hypertexts, much of any familiar narrative schema will not be evident. This can cause difficulties for the readers of a hypertext because they cannot effectively organize the textual information into their situation model. Although readers of hypertexts may not currently be able to rely on a familiar narrative schema, this may change in the future. As hypertexts become more accepted and widespread, writers of hypertext may develop standard rhetorical styles. Readers who are then familiar with those rhetorical styles can use that knowledge to help in their structuring of the information in an effective manner.

The Role of Readers' Abilities.   With the large amount of both high-level and low-level processing that must take place in order to comprehend a text, one can expect differences in comprehension based on the reader's abilities. Skilled readers tend to be better at exploiting context cues and other textual constraints. They are able to make better hypotheses about the meaning of words (Perfetti & Roth, 1981), and are more responsive to the rhetorical structure of the text (Meyer, Brandt, & Bluth, 1980). On the other hand, poor readers' decoding skills are not as effective and instead, they compensate by using context-dependent hypothesis testing. Thus, skilled readers are able to use parallel automatic processing to form better hypotheses about the meaning of the text as they read through it and are not as dependent on the contextual cues of the text. In this manner, if contextual cues are missing or are confusing, then the performance of poor readers will be degraded to an even greater extent.

Skilled readers of linear text are more responsive to the rhetorical structure of the text and possess better decoding skills. In contrast, poor readers must rely more on the context to help in decoding. Hypertext may provide fewer contextual cues than equivalent linear texts. An example is a hypertext in which a reader is not given a lot of information about the structure of the text or about where to go in the text. In a linear text, a poor reader could rely on information from the linear structure for this context, but the same context may not be as evident in the hypertext. On the other hand, a well-structured hypertext that provides a map of its structure may provide additional contextual cues that may not be present in a linear text. In such a case, a poor reader may find the hypertext to be more of an advantage than the equivalent linear text.

Hypertexts also cause an additional processing load by making the reader responsible for navigating the text. Skilled readers, who can process the text automatically, will not have as much interference from the controlled processing task of having to make choices of where to go as they read. Readers with poor reading skills are using a lot more controlled processing and thus will likely have a greater amount of interference from the additional task of navigating the text. This will not let them generate as many hypotheses about the text as they read it, making it harder to integrate the information.

Thus, the abilities of the reader may interact with the type of text format and how that text format is implemented. A well-structured hypertext that does not impose a large navigational load on the reader may be an advantage for poor readers. On the other hand, poor readers may have greater difficulty with a less well-structured hypertext when compared to the equivalent linear text.

Readers' Strategies in Hypertext and Linear Text

Whereas many of the results described earlier were based on tasks in which a reader read through a text in a single linear order, readers also use various strategies for reading through a linear text. Not only do the reader's abilities and the static characteristics of the text determine the comprehension, but also its structural, syntactic, and semantic signals. These signals provide evidence for the macrorelevance of the individual sections of text. A variety of studies have examined the role of different types of text signals on comprehension, including studies of titles (Bransford & Johnson, 1972), frequency of mention (Perfetti & Goldman, 1974), enumeration (Lorch & Chen, 1986), and initial sentences (Kieras, 1981).

These signals not only affect comprehension, but they also determine what a reader looks for in a text and what the reader ignores. A reader may look through a text and find relevant sections based on these signals and skip over sections that do not seem to be as relevant. In this way, a linear text may not always be read linearly. There has been some research on the strategies used in reading a text. However, reading strategies have not been investigated as much as some of the comprehension processes in reading, because there is a lot less control of the conditions, and it is harder to determine what information a subject has read and the subjects' motivations for choosing the particular information from the text.

Goldman and Saul (1990) identified a number of strategies used by subjects when reading text passages. These strategies were identified both at the global level of the text and at the more local levels. Subjects read individual sentences and could go backward and forward through the sentences. At the global level, they identified three approaches; once through, in which subjects read straight through a text; review, in which subjects went to the passage end and then reviewed sentences; and the regress approach, in which they went back to previous sentences throughout the text. They found that subjects almost always used more than one approach in reading a passage. Thus, readers employed a great deal of flexibility in reading the passages. However, their approaches for getting through the text were done in such a manner as to establish both local and global discourse coherence. From these results, they proposed a model of strategy competition for reading strategies. In their model, the choices of where to go in the text followed a set of procedural rules. These procedural rules worked at both the global and local level to maintain coherence of the text, to react to the textual features that served as cues to the coherence relations, and to make strategy choices when coherence could not be established.

Thus, reading is not always a static process that proceeds in a single order. Readers can employ a variety of strategies for proceeding through a text. These strategies may be determined by a variety of factors, including the reader's knowledge for the domain, the reader's goals, the reader's skills, and the characteristics of the text. However, the reader must still work to maintain the overriding goal of proceeding through the text in a coherent manner.

The examination of strategies in hypertext has primarily concentrated on the search strategies of readers when hypertexts have been used as information retrieval systems. Because hypertexts provide additional navigational flexibility to readers, one could expect that readers would employ a variety of strategies. As evident from the Goldman and Saul (1990) study, readers use a variety of strategies in order to maintain coherence in a linear text. It is expected that readers of hypertexts would do the same, as they must maintain coherence in order to develop a coherent mental representation of the text.

Part of the goal of developing hypertexts is to have mechanisms to simplify the navigational strategies of readers. Hypertexts were developed so that readers could get to the relevant sections in a more efficient manner than in linear texts. For this reason, it is expected that the strategies of the reader can depend greatly on what mechanisms are implemented in the hypertext. A hypertext based primarily on search will tend to structure a reader's strategies to using search. However, these mechanisms must also match the goals of the reader and these goals can influence the choice of strategies. Hypertext typically permits a reader to see more of the structure of the text and therefore can make it somewhat easier to find the relevant places in the text. Thus, the reading strategies in hypertext could be expanded from those found in reading a linear text and could depend on the mechanisms provided in the hypertext and on the goals of the reader.

TWO EXPERIMENTS APPLYING TEXT COMPREHENSION TO HYPERTEXT

Overall, there are a variety of factors that can cause differences in readers' comprehension and strategies of a text written in hypertext and linear form. Foltz (1993) ran two experiments that focused on two of these factors, the coherence of the text and how the goals of the reader affected reading strategies. The first experiment examined the comprehension and strategies of readers using either a linear text or one of two hypertext environments. The second experiment used verbal reports to investigate readers' strategies in hypertext.

A Comparison of Linear Text and Hypertext

In the first experiment, readers' comprehension and strategies were measured when using either a linear text or one of two hypertext versions of a chapter from an undergraduate level economics textbook. The goals of the readers were manipulated so that half of the readers read the chapter for general knowledge, whereas the other half read the chapter in order to find certain specific pieces of information.

One of the purposes of the experiment was to determine whether there were differences in readers' comprehension and strategies between the hypertext and the linear text. It was hypothesized that because readers had little background knowledge on the subject of the text, the lack of coherence in the hypertext would adversely affect the readers' comprehension when compared to the comprehension of the readers of the linear text. A second objective was to determine whether the goals of the reader interacted with the format of the text. More specifically, did readers use different strategies based on their goals, and did one format of the text afford better comprehension than another? It was hypothesized that hypertext may be more suited for tasks involving information search, so readers with specific goals, in which they must find the relevant information, may perform better on the hypertext, whereas readers with general reading goals would find an advantage for the linear text, as it presented a single coherent set of information on the text.

An undergraduate level economics textbook chapter was converted into a hypertext using guidelines from several works on hypertext (e.g., Martin, 1990; Nielsen, 1990; Shneiderman, 1987). This included using the authors' section titles to designate nodes and the authors' outline for generating a hierarchy. The resulting hierarchical hypertext contained 6,018 words consisting of 26 nodes. In addition to the hierarchical structure, there were also 17 cross links where the authors made references to other sections. The hypertext permitted readers to navigate through the text using buttons to follow both the hierarchical structure and the cross links. In addition, there was a map of the hypertext structure, which permitted jumping to any point in the text.

As described earlier, one of the hypothesized problems with hypertext may be that the jumps from node to node do not present as coherent a chapter as that of the linear text, resulting in lower comprehension. In order to investigate this idea, a second, more coherent hypertext was also developed. This hypertext was exactly the same as the first one, but it also provided additional coherence in the text by automatically modifying the text in order to make it more coherent. To determine when a noncoherent jump was made in the hypertext, a macropropositional analysis of the text was first performed. In this analysis, the text was reduced to a set of macropropositions, describing the gist of each sentence. The analysis indicated where possible noncoherent jumps would occur while reading the hypertext and what missing pieces of information would be needed for any jump in order to make the transition more coherent. Then, whenever noncoherent jumps were made, the computer added an additional first paragraph of the necessary missing macropropositions in sentence form, in order to make the transition more coherent. An example of one of the hypertext nodes with the inserted coherence paragraph, labeled "General Background" is shown in Fig. 6.1. In order to compare the hypertexts to a linear version of the text, an online linear version was created. This text permitted subjects to turn pages back and forth through the text and allowed them to go to the start and end of the chapter. A table of contents was also provided as the first page of the chapter. This table of contents was equivalent to the hierarchical representation presented in the hypertext map.

Undergraduate subjects with no background in economics read one of the three text formats. Half of the readers were told to find specific information in

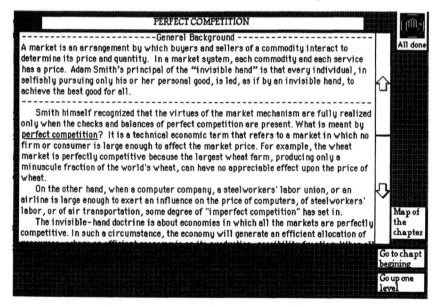

FIG. 6.1. Node from coherent hypertext with context paragraph inserted.

the text that was distributed across several sections, whereas the other half of the readers read the text for general knowledge. After reading the text, the subjects answered comprehension questions and wrote an essay on the chapter. Some of the questions required subjects to recall information from the text, whereas other questions required subjects to use what they had learned from the text and apply it to new examples. This permitted an evaluation of both what they remembered from the text and what they learned from the text.

The surprising results of the study were that very few performance differences existed between the readers of the hypertexts and the linear text. There were no differences between text formats for the amount of time it took subjects to read the text. The subjects' comprehension also was equivalent for the different text formats. There were no differences in the number of macropropositions subjects generated in their essay and no differences in the subjects' scores on the short answer essay and multiple choice test. However, subjects who used the hypertexts did score better on questions that assessed their knowledge of the structure of the text. There were also no significant performance differences between the two types of hypertexts.

Manipulating the goals of the reader did have an effect. Subjects searching for the specific information in the text were faster but showed lower comprehension on the general knowledge questions. However, these measures did not interact with type of text, indicating that different types of text format did not differentially affect the comprehension of readers with different reading goals. Thus, the hypertexts were of no greater help to the readers than the linear text in their search for information.

These results are similar to other studies in finding few comprehension differences between hypertext and linear text. However, in order to understand the lack of differences, it is important to look at readers' strategies. The computer kept a log of each subjects' progress and section choices as they read through the text. This permitted an analysis of the strategies that the subjects used for getting through the text and a characterization of the order in which they read the text. Any node or page on which a subject spent more than 5 seconds was counted as being read by the subject. Thus, in the linear text, subjects could still make noncoherent transitions by quickly paging forward or backward. The order that the subjects read the text was then compared to a macropropositional analysis of the text in order to count the number of coherent transitions made by the subjects. A coherent transition was one that did not violate the macrostructure of the text (i.e., the context of the node they were reading was similar to the context of the node to which they jumped).

For all groups in the study, 80 to 90% of the transitions were made in a manner that was coherent with respect to the macrostructure of the text. There were no differences due to text format or readers' goals. Although this is not a surprising result for readers of the linear text, it suggests that readers of the hypertext made transitions primarily within the same context and seldom used any features to move them into very different parts of the hypertext. This coherence measure also correlated with the number of macropropositions generated in the subjects' essays indicating that the more coherently the text was read, the better the essay. Thus, the readers' comprehension of the hypertext was better if the reader chose to go through it in a coherent manner. The fact that there were no group differences in the coherent transition measure suggests that the lack of comprehension differences between the three text formats could be due to ceiling effects. All subjects were seeing approximately the same text in about an equivalently coherent manner, and thus, their comprehension would not differ greatly. These coherence results therefore indicate that subjects tended to use a very rational approach of getting through the hypertexts, trying to maintain coherence.

Verbal Reports of Hypertext Readers Strategies

The results from Experiment 1 showed that, although there were few differences in comprehension due to the three text formats, the reading strategies used by the subjects were all very similar. This indicates that subjects used heuristics to employ information from the text to guide them through the text in a coherent manner. While Experiment 1 showed evidence of these strategies, it did not provide data that showed the reasons why the subjects used these strategies and what type of information from the text helped them to use these strategies. In the second experiment, verbal protocols (e.g., Ericsson & Simon, 1984) were collected about readers' strategies from six subjects as they read through the hypertext. In this experiment, two of the subjects read through the hypertext with instructions to find specific information, whereas the other four subjects read for general knowledge. Subjects were instructed to read the texts silently, but to describe out loud everything they were thinking as they read through the texts. If at any point the subjects were silent and were not reading, and when they made any transition in the hypertext, the experimenter prompted them to describe what they were thinking. The results therefore provided a qualitative measure of subjects' reasoning about their navigation strategies.

The verbal protocols indicated that subjects seldom wanted to stray from the hierarchical structure and they expressed interest in reading all the text in one area of the hypertext before moving on to other areas.

For example, one subject said, "I think I'm done in government. I've covered all, covered that. Uhuh, I'm going to go to . . . how markets solve the basic economic problems" (Foltz, 1993, p. 84). This strategy has somewhat of the same effect as the depth-first strategy. By reading one part of the hierarchy before moving on to other parts, the subject avoids moving out of the current context at any point. Indeed, if this strategy is applied recursively, the two strategies are equivalent.

Subjects with the general reading goals used reading strategies for covering the whole text in a coherent manner. However, when they made noncoherent transitions, they often expressed confusion and then tried to get back to where they had been previously. On the other hand, the subjects with specific reading goals tried to maintain the context around the specific information they needed to find.

> Um, I was mostly looking at the general topics and trying not to skip, go all the way down to the, that in case there might be other topics to the left that were on the same kind of hierarchy, or whatever. I tried to look at, get an overview of those other three before I went over to there, in case they had something to do with that. . . . I just think I needed an overview of the little things around it in order to get at the answers to that question. (Foltz, 1993, p. 84)

Thus, it was not sufficient to find the relevant information in the text. In order for that information to make sense, the subject needed background context that could be provided by reading the text from the nodes that were around the relevant node. In addition, based on their time-stamped record, when subjects were instructed to read with a goal of finding particular pieces of information, rather than using jumps in the hypertext to go down to the specific information, they tended to start at the upper level nodes above the desired information and then work their way down to the specific information they had to read. They indicated that this gave them the appropriate background context.

The verbal protocols showed that subjects used strategies for maintaining the coherence of the text. It was also important to know what information they used to help guide them to use these reading strategies. From both the verbal protocols and the time-stamped record of actions, subjects seemed to rely primarily on the map to guide their strategies. Subjects consulted the map an average of 8 times throughout the session. This indicated that they used the map often to help orient themselves. The subjects' protocols also showed that they relied on the map for guidance. For example, one subject said, "I'm thinking umm, I'm trying to decide whether to go back to the map of the chapter and work my way over actually to keep working my way down the map" (Foltz, 1993, p. 85). In addition to the verbalizations about the map, subjects also appeared to use the titles of nodes to guide them. One subject identified the three nodes under the node titled, "The three functions of government," and decided he had better cover all three functions. Thus, although the map of the hierarchical structure appeared to be the primary piece of information used to guide the subjects, the titles also identified relationships between items in the hierarchy and allowed the subjects to navigate by following the labels.

These results corroborate the results found in Experiment 1. The results show that reading a hypertext is not just a reading process, but also a process of problem solving. In order to understand the text, subjects developed heuristics for maintaining coherence with an unfamiliar text domain and text format. The verbal protocols showed that the subjects were aware of their strategies to read the information around one area of the hierarchy before moving on to other areas.

In this manner, their strategies allowed them to always stay within the same textual context.

IMPLICATIONS FOR HYPERTEXT AND LINEAR TEXT

Reading Strategies and Comprehension in Hypertext

Despite the differences in the text formats, in the previous experiments, subjects used strategies to navigate the texts in a coherent manner. The similar approaches to reading the text resulted in similar amounts of text comprehension for the different text formats. For navigating the linear text, subjects merely relied on the linear order of the text for following the coherent path. For the hypertexts, subjects relied on additional constraints in the text such as the map and node titles which signaled the structure of the text. These signals served as guides for locating additional nodes that would flow coherently with the previously read nodes.

Manipulating the goals of the reader changed the readers' strategies. Readers with the specific goals saw fewer nodes and pages of the text and read for a shorter amount of time. However, although they were supposed to find information that was in separate places in the hierarchy, there were no differences in the number of coherent transitions made based on the readers' goals. This indicates that even when readers need to find specific information in an unfamiliar text, they still may need to have the appropriate background context. The verbal protocols from Experiment 2 confirmed that although subjects were aware of where the relevant nodes were, they read down to those nodes in order to put the relevant nodes in the appropriate context. In addition, the goal manipulation did not interact with the text format. Thus, even though subjects had different reading goals, they employed similar reading strategies on the different text formats.

The modified version of the hypertext that provided additional coherence showed no real differences from the original hypertext. Subjects may have ignored the added information that was provided to them by the coherent hypertext. However, based on the strategies used by the subjects in Experiment 1 and on the protocols in Experiment 2, the general background context provided by the coherent hypertext appears to be the type of information that the subjects needed to maintain coherence and to provide a context for what they were currently reading. Thus, subjects may not have noticed this information sufficiently or ignored it when it appeared. It is also possible that not enough information was provided in these "background context" paragraphs to be efficiently used. However, because subjects tended to navigate the coherent hypertext in a coherent manner, this information was also seldom presented to them. Thus, there may not have been enough opportunities for them to use the background context provided to produce significant differences between the hypertexts. Although this research failed to show that the automatic coherence aided the readers, this type of approach may be of use to hypertexts. Given the right type of information in these background context paragraphs and proper training of the readers, readers would not have had to rely as much on following coherent paths. Instead, they could use the background context provided to give them the necessary coherence when making jumps out of a particular context.

The strategies used by the subjects show evidence for the dominance of global comprehension in reading. The subjects used a rational approach to reading, maintaining an order of reading that was consistent with the macrostructure of the text. Even when the structure of the text had been modified from its linear form, they chose paths through the text that would flow coherently. This was consistent with the readers' goals to form a coherent macrostructure. Thus, readers of a hypertext are opportunistic. They look for the cues that will lead them to the most coherent path through the text. This behavior is also consistent with the rules for coherent reading strategies set forth in Goldman and Saul (1990).

With readers using rules to maintain coherence, this means that readers must develop a set of rules and then choose what rules to use for different situations. In this way, reading becomes an application of problem solving. The problem of navigating a hypertext coherently is similar to searching in a problem space in an unfamiliar domain (e.g., Newell, 1980; Newell & Simon, 1972). The reader has a set of possible actions for getting through the text (problem space) and a set of search methods for finding the most effective paths through the text. Because the subjects in this experiment were all expert readers, they had fairly powerful search methods for discovering coherent relationships. However, the subjects were all in an unfamiliar text domain (economics), which put some limits on their ability to use their search methods to find the most coherent path.

This approach to navigating through the hypertext is also consistent with investigations of exploratory learning in computer systems, such as the CE+ model of Lewis and Polson (1990). Their model of behavior in unfamiliar computer domains uses a label following, hill climbing search method in order to choose the relevant actions. In label following (e.g., Engelbeck, 1986), the user's goals are matched with the possible actions, and an action is chosen based on the degree of overlap in terms between the two. The label following heuristic is similar to the methods the hypertext readers used for determining where to make the next coherent transition. For finding specific information, subjects could match their reading goals to the possible nodes they could read to identify relevant nodes of the text and then work their way down to the appropriate nodes. For subjects with general reading goals, they could use the titles as guides for determining the relationships between nodes in order to determine what transitions would be the most coherent.

The Lewis and Polson research suggests that one of the keys to aiding in problem solving is to design for successful guessing (see also, Norman 1986, 1988). This is a similar necessity for hypertexts. A reader of a hypertext must be able to guess whether following a particular link will lead toward the relevant information and also be coherent with the current context. In order for a reader to make these successful guesses, this information needs to be evident through the structure of the text and the titles of the nodes.

Text Comprehension Theory and Hypertext

Although one of the original goals of this research was to determine the effect of the text's coherence on readers of hypertexts and linear texts, the results suggest that the similar coherence strategies overshadowed the effects of the text formats. In linear text, coherence is a good predictor of comprehension (e.g., Kintsch & Vipond, 1979; van Dijk & Kintsch, 1983). In this research, comprehension was equivalent because the resulting coherence of the text formats was equivalent. Even when modifying the goals of the reader, the text was still read coherently, resulting in few comprehension differences. Thus, due to a lack of variability in coherence, this research cannot draw conclusions about how much the coherence can break down in a hypertext and thereby affect the comprehension.

Readers' strategies indicate the strong role coherence plays in reading a hypertext. In the development of hypertext, the coherence between linked nodes is not often considered. Hypertext guidelines tell creators to link related items, however, there are few guidelines that tell them to make the text of linked nodes cohere. It is typically assumed that because two nodes are linked by some common piece of information, the reader can then generate the correct inferences about the link and incorporate the new information into his or her representation of the text. The results of this study show that subjects avoided the cases of "loosely" linked information (e.g., cross-hierarchical links), and instead, primarily made transitions to highly related nodes.

It should be noted that this research examined the strategies of readers who were not familiar with the domain of the text. The results could change greatly with readers who are knowledgeable of the domain. With more background knowledge, readers could perform better problem solving to choose better coherent paths through the text. These readers would have the correct knowledge to make informed guesses on where to go in the text. With the proper knowledge structures, they could also make noncoherent jumps without adverse effects because they would possess the appropriate background knowledge to make the necessary bridging inferences. Thus, although readers with little background knowledge of the text domain may have to rely on coherent paths in order to read through the text, a knowledgeable reader may be better able to exploit some of the less coherent links in the hypertext.

Implications for the Design of Hypertexts

The results of these studies indicate that text comprehension theory can provide predictions for the design of hypertexts. Based on the theory, the primary design issues are to consider the type of text, how it will be used, and who will be using it. These issues can affect both what the reader can learn from the text and the type of strategies the reader will employ. In the case of these studies, the text was designed primarily for students to study concepts in economics. Students reading the text had little background knowledge on the topic and had the goals of either reading through the text or of searching for information in the text. Thus, these results cannot be generalized to all hypertexts in all situations.

One of the primary considerations in the design of a hypertext should be to focus on the readers' strategies. These strategies can vary, depending both on the goals of the reader and the background knowledge of the reader. A reader who wants to find specific information in a hypertext needs to have simple methods to locate that information. However, having the specific information without the appropriate background context can be useless. Thus, for hypertexts it is not just a matter of getting a reader to the correct place in the text, but also ensuring that the relevant information is represented in a meaningful context. The results from Experiment 2 indicated that subjects finding specific information needed the appropriate background context before they could go ahead and read the specific information.

For readers with extensive background knowledge, text comprehension theory predicts that this meaningful context may not be needed. However, for readers without the proper background knowledge, the additional information will be more valuable. For this reason, it would make sense to insert the appropriate context, or permit the novice reader to read through all the background context in order to get the relevant information. This concept is somewhat similar to the idea of "guided tours" in hypertexts in which an author provides a single path through the text with the appropriate context (e.g., Marshall & Irish, 1989). It is also similar to the "training wheels" methodology for interfaces which kept novices on the correct path, only allowing them the use of a subset of the available functions (e.g., Carroll & Carrithers, 1984).

In addition to providing an appropriate context for readers, it is important to support familiar reading strategies. Readers will navigate through the text trying to find coherent paths. Thus, readers should be able to identify these paths. This can be done is several ways. Providing a clear structure of the text will aid the reader in finding these paths. Although a large text may have an enormous structure that cannot be visualized as a whole, providing local information around the current node will provide both additional context for the reader and additional information as to what nodes will produce a coherent representation.

Along with having a clear structure, providing good labels for the nodes will also aid readers. Because novice readers tend to use a label following strategy, labels that clearly indicate the role of a particular node will help the reader in successfully guessing the appropriate coherent path (e.g., Lewis & Polson, 1990). Support for successful guessing in a hypertext should be similar to that of using a standard rhetorical structure in linear text. Readers who are familiar with the structure will be able to exploit it to their advantage. Those who are unfamiliar with it will have to expend cognitive effort in problem solving at the expense of the primary task of comprehending the information from the text.

One of the common tasks in developing hypertext is converting a linear text into a hypertext. Although changing a text to a hypertext may provide a lot more flexibility to the readers, these conversions typically concentrate on restructuring the information rather than making large scale changes to the text. A converted linear text may still contain many of the ordering signals that were in the original text. These signals could include such text factors as enumeration and the mention of information that occurred previously in the linear text. These factors may cause the text to be read in the same linear fashion as the original text. The text may also have to be modified in order to improve its coherence. Restructuring a text will cause more possible ways to get to any particular node. The text in that node will have to be written in such a way that a jump into that node will be coherent. Thus, the conversion of a linear text to a well-written hypertext can involve an extensive amount of modification of the original text in order for the text to be more appropriate in a hypertext format.

One way around the problem of structuring when converting a text to hypertext is to keep the text in the linear form. SuperBook (Egan et al., 1989; Landauer et al., 1993) uses such an approach. The text is kept in its original form, but also enhanced through a variety of features to facilitate navigation. These features include a dynamic table of contents, a fisheye view of the current context, and a search that posts the hits against the table of contents. This permits readers to get to the relevant places in the text efficiently but also permits them to read the text linear order.

One of the current difficulties in developing a hypertext is that hypertext writing environments are still in their infancy. Improved environments will help a writer see the constraints of the text as the text is developed. Such features will permit the writer to be better able to consider the coherence of the text from the node and how the text should best be structured.

Thus, developing a hypertext is not just a matter of developing a text with all relevant interconnections. Instead, an effective hypertext must be based on a coherent structure. This structure must present an interface to the reader that will make the reader's strategies simple to use.

Future Issues for Text and Hypertext Research

The studies just described show the importance that readers place on maintaining the coherence of the text as they navigate a hypertext, however, there remain many research issues that still must be explored in hypertexts. These results, and many other studies indicate that hypertexts, as they are currently implemented, are not suitable for all reading applications.

This research sought to identify the effect of differences in the amount of coherence in the hypertext and the linear text, however, the strategies of the readers created equivalent amounts of coherent transitions. Not all hypertexts would permit subjects to perform as many coherent transitions as the hypertext used in this research. Thus, it would be instrumental to evaluate hypertexts that cause a greater amount of noncoherent transitions in order to determine how much the coherence affects the comprehension. An alternative is to examine hypertexts that have large amounts of coherence. Hypertexts based on rhetorical models, such as systems for argumentation, enforce the coherence to a large extent. An analysis of reading comprehension on such systems may find that they produce larger amounts of comprehension and also provide a more appropriate representation of arguments than the equivalent linear version.

Modeling Text and Hypertext Readability.   Models of text comprehension (e.g., van Dijk & Kintsch, 1983) can be applied to hypertext as well as to linear text. In both cases, the key is to be able to measure the appropriateness of the text's structures and the resulting human representation of those structures. The primary difference between the current text comprehension models for linear text and those for the hypertext is that a model for hypertext must also take into account the reader's behavior as he or she navigates through the text. In this way, the model must not only take into account the text, but also the reader's strategies for dealing with the computer interface (e.g., Lewis & Polson, 1990). A model of hypertext comprehension must consider both the information the reader gains from the text and how that information can affect the readers' choice of strategies for proceeding through the text. Thus, this involves both an understanding of the constraints of the text and of the constraints of the user interface. Given a successful model of these factors, we can generate better guidelines on how to develop more readable hypertexts that support more successful reading strategies.

Where Can Hypertext Succeed?.   From many of the studies in the field of hypertext, hypertexts have often performed worse, or just as well as the equivalent linear text. This raises the question: What are the areas where a hypertext will be more successful than a linear text, and what sorts of features will the hypertext need for this success? One of the remaining problems of paper texts is still the fact that their indices are inadequate and unwieldy to use. A current success for hypertext is as a search engine. Although this blurs the distinction between information retrieval systems and hypertexts, the ability to search through a text simplifies many tasks. Hypertexts, such as SuperBook, permit readers to find the relevant information in an efficient manner. Although current computer indexing methods still leave much room for improvement (e.g., Dumais, 1988), the ability to move from one piece of relevant information to another cannot be matched in equivalent paper versions of large amounts of text.

A second area where there is a great deal of potential for hypertext systems is in representing textual information that is not as easily presented in linear form. Such domains as legal argumentation and design knowledge have such problems. Any piece of textual information can have many related arguments and counterarguments. These can be represented graphically with links between the arguments. Because the arguments are designed to follow each other, the links are constrained to be coherent. Thus, the reader of the hypertext may follow the links and still get a coherent representation of the information. Although these systems may provide an advantage to the reader, they do put a large load on the writer. Unlike preparing a single coherent set of arguments, the writer must determine the relationship between all pieces of information and structure them in a much more complicated manner than the linear equivalent. In the future, better computerized methods based on models of the text may be able to do some of this structuring, simplifying the task of the writer.

A third potential area for success in hypertexts is suggested by the investigation in this research of providing dynamic coherence to the hypertext. The goal of dynamic coherence is to provide additional information to the reader so that the text automatically contains information that is more appropriate to the reader's representation of the text. Readers of a text will bring large differences in reading abilities and background knowledge to a text. Through modeling the reader's knowledge, abilities, and goals, hypertexts could be developed that perform dynamic structuring of the text. These hypertexts could include additional background knowledge to readers with little knowledge and make the text more coherent for readers with low reading abilities. For readers with general reading goals or who are trying to get an overview, the text could be presented with a single path. For readers trying to find specific information, the text could provide search capabilities and appropriate background context of any relevant items.

Although the concept of personalized text sounds like a wonderful idea, accurately gauging the readers background knowledge, abilities, and goals can be difficult. A lot of this will depend on being able to develop appropriate user models. These models would need to include information about what is contained in the text, what information a reader already knows, and what information the reader needs to know.

Success for hypertexts lies in exploiting the powers of both the computer and the writer to generate better personalized texts. However, in order to do this, we must first have accurate models of such factors as what a reader knows, what a reader needs, what methods a reader can use, and what information is contained in the text. Thus, the future of hypertext depends on improving both models of the user and models of the text.

ACKNOWLEDGMENTS

The author thanks Walter Kintsch, Peter Polson, Anders Ericsson, Reid Hastie, and Gerhard Fischer for their advice and comments on this project. He also thanks Adrienne Lee, Thomas Landauer, Susan Dumais, and Dennis Egan for their help. Support was provided by grants from the Army Research Institute ARI project MDA 903-86-CO143, the National Institute of Health, and Bell Communications Research.

REFERENCES

Begoray, J. A. (1990). An introduction to hypermedia issues, systems and application areas. *International Journal of Man–Machine Studies, 33*, 121–147.

Black, J. B., & Bower, G. H. (1979). Episodes as chunks in narrative memory. *Journal of Verbal Learning and Verbal Behavior, 18*, 309–318.

Bolter, J. D. (1991). *Writing space: The computer, hypertext, and the history of writing*. Hillsdale, NJ: Lawrence Erlbaum Associates.

Botafogo, R. A., & Shneiderman, B. (1991). Identifying aggregates in hypertext structures. In J. Walker (Ed.), *Proceedings of Hypertext '91* (pp. 63–74). San Antonio, TX: ACM.

Bransford, J. D., & Franks, J. J. (1971). The abstraction of linguistic ideas. *Cognitive Psychology, 2*, 331–350.

Bransford, J. D., & Johnson, M. K. (1972). Contextual prerequisites for understanding: Some investigations of comprehension and recall. *Journal of Verbal Learning and Verbal Behavior, 11*, 717–726.

Britton, B. K., & Glynn, S. M. (1989). *Computer writing environments: Theory, research, and design*. Hillsdale, NJ: Lawrence Erlbaum Associates.

Britton, B. K., & Gulgoz, S. (1991). Using Kintsch's computational model to improve instructional text: Effects of repairing inference calls on recall and cognitive structures. *Journal of Educational Psychology, 83*, 329–345.

Britton, B. K., Meyer, B. J., Hodge, M. H., & Glynn, S. M. (1980). Effects of the organization of text on memory: Tests of retrieval and response criterion hypotheses. *Journal of Experimental Psychology: Human Learning and Memory, 6*(5), 620–629.

Card, S., Moran, T. P., & Newell, A. (1983). *The psychology of human–computer interaction*. Hillsdale, NJ: Lawrence Erlbaum Associates.

Carroll, J. M., & Carrithers, C. (1984). Training wheels in a user interface. *Communications of the ACM, 27*(8), 800–806.

Charney, D. (1987). Comprehending non-linear text: The role of discourse cues and reading strategies. In S. Weiss & M. Schwartz (Eds.), *Proceedings of Hypertext '87* (pp. 109–120). Chapel Hill: ACM.

Charney, D. (1994). The impact of hypertext on processes of reading and writing. In S. J. Hilligoss & C. L. Selfe (Eds.), *Literacy and Computers*. New York: MLA.

Conklin, J., & Begeman, M. L. (1989). gIBIS: A tool for all reasons. *Journal of the American Society for Information Science, 40*(3), 200–213.

Croft, W. B., & Turtle, H. (1989). A retrieval model incorporating hypertext links. In F. Halasz & N. Meyrowitz (Eds.), *Proceedings of Hypertext '89* (pp. 213–224). Pittsburgh: ACM.

Crouch, D. B., Crouch, C. J., & Andreas, G. (1989). The use of cluster hierarchies in hypertext information retrieval. In F. Halasz & N. Meyrowitz (Eds.), *Proceedings of Hypertext '89* (pp. 225–238). Pittsburgh: ACM.

Dillon, A. (1991). Readers' models of text structures: The case of academic articles. *International Journal of Man–Machine Studies, 35*, 913–925.

Doane, S., Kintsch, W., & Polson, P. G. (1989). Action planning: Producing UNIX commands. In *Proceedings of the 11th annual meeting of the Cognitive Science Society* (pp. 458–465). Hillsdale, NJ: Lawrence Erlbaum Associates.

Dumais, S. T. (1988). Textual information retrieval. In M. Helander (Ed.), *Handbook of human-computer interaction* (pp. 673–700). New York: Elsevier.

Egan, D. E., Remde, J. R., Gomez, L. M., Landauer, T. K., Eberhardt, J., & Lochbaum, C. C. (1989). Formative design-evaluation of SuperBook. *Transactions on Information Systems, 7*(1), 30–57.

Engelbeck, G. E. (1986). *Exceptions to generalizations: Implications for formal models of human-computer interaction.* Unpublished master's thesis, University of Colorado, Boulder.

Ericsson, K. A., & Simon, H. A. (1984). *Protocol analysis: Verbal reports as data.* Cambridge, MA: MIT Press.

Fincher-Kiefer, R., Post, T. A., Greene, T. R., & Voss, J. F. (1988). On the role of prior knowledge and task demands in the processing of text. *Journal of Memory and Language, 27,* 416–428.

Fischer, G., McCall, R., & Morch, A. (1989). JANUS: Integrating hypertext with a knowledge-based design environment. In F. Halasz & N. Meyrowitz (Eds.), *Proceedings of Hypertext '89* (pp. 105–118). Pittsburgh: ACM.

Fodor, J. D., Fodor, J. A., & Garrett, M. F. (1975). The psychological unreality of semantic representations. *Linguistic Inquiry, 6,* 515–531.

Foltz, P. W. (1993). *Readers' comprehension and strategies in linear text and hypertext.* Unpublished doctoral dissertation, University of Colorado, Boulder.

Furuta, R., & Stotts, P. D. (1989). Programming browsing semantics in Trellis. In F. Halasz & N. Meyrowitz (Eds.), *Proceedings of Hypertext '89* (pp. 27–42). Pittsburgh: ACM.

Goldman, S. R., & Saul, E. U. (1990). Flexibility in text processing: A strategy competition model. *Learning and Individual Differences, 2*(2), 181–219.

Gould, J. D., Alfaro, L., Fonn, R., Haupt, B., Minuto, A., & Salaun, J. (1987). Why reading was slower from CRT displays than from paper. In *Proceedings of the ACM CHI + GI '87* (pp. 7–11). Toronto, Canada: ACM.

Gould, J. D., & Grischkowsky, N. (1984). Doing the same work with hard copy and with cathode ray tube (CRT) computer terminals. *Human Factors, 26,* 296–300.

Hammond, N., & Allinson, L. (1989). Extending hypertext for learning: An investigation of access and guidance tools. In A. Sutcliffe & L. Macauley (Eds.), *Proceedings of the HCI '89 Conference on People and Computers V* (pp. 293–304). Nottingham, UK: Cambridge University Press.

Hardman, L., & Sharrat, B. (1989). User-centered hypertext design: The application of HCI design principles and guidelines. In R. McAleese & C. Green (Eds.), *Proceedings of State of the Art Hypertext 2* (pp. 252–259). York, UK: Blackwell Scientific Publications.

Kieras, D. E. (1981). The role of major referents and sentence topic in the construction of passage macrostructure. *Discourse Processes, 4,* 1–15.

Kieras, D. E., & Polson, P. G. (1985). An approach to the formal analysis of user complexity. *International Journal of Man-Machine Studies, 22,* 365–394.

Kintsch, W. (1974). *The representation of meaning in memory.* Hillsdale, NJ: Lawrence Erlbaum Associates.

Kintsch, W. (1988). The use of knowledge in discourse processing: A construction-integration model. *Psychological Review, 95,* 363–394.

Kintsch, W., & Keenan, J. M. (1973). Reading rate and retention as a function of the number of propositions in base structure of sentences. *Cognitive Psychology, 5,* 257–274.

Kintsch, W., & van Dijk, T. A. (1978). Toward a model of text comprehension and production. *Psychological Review, 85,* 363–394.

Kintsch, W., & Vipond, D. (1979). Reading comprehension and readability in educational practice and psychological theory. In L. G. Nilsson (Ed.), *Perspectives on memory research* (pp. 329–365). Hillsdale, NJ: Lawrence Erlbaum Associates.

Landauer, T. K., Egan, D., Remde, J., Lesk, M. J., Lochbaum, C. C., & Ketchum, D. (1993). Enhancing the usability of text through computer delivery and formative evaluation: The SuperBook project. In C. McKnight, A. Dillon, & J. Richardson (Eds.), *Hypertext: A psychological perspective.* New York: E. Horwood.

Landow, G. P. (1989). Hypertext in literary education, criticism, and scholarship. *Computers and the Humanities, 23*, 173–198.

Lewis, C., & Polson, P. G. (1990). Theory-based design for easily learned interfaces. *HCI, 5*, 191–220.

Lorch, R. F., & Chen, A. H. (1986). Effects of number signals on reading and recall. *Journal of Educational Psychology, 78*, 263–279.

Mannes, S., & Kintsch, W. (1991). Routine computing tasks: Planning as understanding. *Cognitive Science, 15*, 305–342.

Marchionini, G., & Shneiderman, B. (1987). Finding facts vs. browsing knowledge in hypertext systems. *IEEE Computer, 21*(1), 70–80.

Marshall, C. C., & Irish, P. M. (1989). Guided tours and on-line presentations: How authors make existing hypertext intelligible for readers. In F. Halasz & N. Meyrowitz (Eds.), *Proceedings of Hypertext '89* (pp. 15–26). Pittsburgh: ACM.

Martin, J. (1990). *Hyperdocuments and how to create them.* Englewood Cliffs, NJ: Prentice-Hall.

Meyer, B. J. F. (1973). *The organization of prose and its effects on memory.* Amsterdam: North Holland.

Meyer, B. J. F., Brandt, D. M., & Bluth, G. J. (1980). Use of top-level structure in text: Key for reading comprehension in ninth-grade students. *Reading Research Quarterly, 16*, 72–103.

Miller, J. R., & Kintsch, W. (1980). Readability and recall of short prose passages: A theoretical analysis. *Journal of Experimental Psychology: Human Learning and Memory, 6*(4), 335–354.

Monk, A. F., Walsh, P., & Dix, A. J. (1988). A comparison of hypertext, scrolling, and folding as mechanisms for program browsing. In D. M. Jones & R. Winder (Eds.), *People and Computers IV* (pp. 421–435). Cambridge, England: Cambridge University Press.

Nelson, T. (1967). Getting it out of our system. In G. Schechter (Ed.), *Information retrieval: A critical review* (pp. 191–210). Washington, DC: Thompson Books.

Newell, A. (1980). Reasoning, problem solving and decision processes: The problem space as a fundamental category. In R. Nickerson (Ed.), *Attention and performance VIII* (pp. 693–718). Hillsdale, NJ: Lawrence Erlbaum Associates.

Newell, A., & Simon, H. A. (1972). *Human problem solving.* Englewood Cliffs, NJ: Prentice-Hall.

Nielsen, J. (1989). The matters that really matter for hypertext usability. In F. Halasz & N. Meyrowitz (Eds.), *Proceedings of Hypertext '89* (pp. 239–248). Pittsburgh: ACM.

Nielsen, J. (1990). *Hypertext and hypermedia.* San Diego, CA: Academic Press.

Norman, D. A. (1986). Cognitive engineering. In D. A. Norman & S. W. Draper (Eds.), *User centered system design: New perspectives in human-computer interaction* (pp. 31–61). Hillsdale, NJ: Lawrence Erlbaum Associates.

Norman, D. A. (1988). *The psychology of everyday things.* New York: Basic Books.

Perfetti, C. A., & Goldman, S. R. (1974). Thematization of sentence retrieval. *Journal of Verbal Learning and Verbal Behavior, 13*, 70–79.

Perfetti, C. A., & Roth, S. (1981). Some of the interactive processes in reading and their role in reading skill. In A. Lesgold & C. Perfetti (Eds.), *Interactive processes in reading* (pp. 269–297). Hillsdale, NJ: Lawrence Erlbaum Associates.

Poulsen, D., Kintsch, E., Kintsch, W., & Premack, D. (1979). Children's comprehension and memory for stories. *Journal of Experimental Child Psychology, 28*, 379–403.

Shneiderman, B. (1987). User interface design and evaluation for an electronic encyclopedia. In G. Salvendy (Eds.), *Cognitive engineering in the design of human-computer interaction and expert systems* (pp. 207–223). New York: Elsevier.

Spilich, G. J., Vesonder, G. T., Chiesi, H. L., & Voss, J. F. (1979). Text processing of domain-related information for individuals with high and low domain knowledge. *Journal of Verbal Learning and Verbal Behavior, 18*, 275–290.

Spiro, R. J., & Jehng, J. C. (1990). Cognitive flexibility and hypertext: Theory and technology for the nonlinear and multidimensional traversal of complex subject matter. In D. Nix & R. J. Spiro (Eds.), *Cognition, education and multimedia: Exploring ideas in high technology.* Hillsdale, NJ: Lawrence Erlbaum Associates.

van Dijk, T. A., & Kintsch, W. (1983). *Strategies of discourse comprehension.* New York: Academic Press.

Voss, J. F., Vesonder, G. T., & Spilich, G. J. (1980). Text generation and recall by high-knowledge and low-knowledge subjects. *Journal of Verbal Learning and Verbal Behavior, 19,* 651–667.

Weyer, S. A. (1982). The design of a dynamic book for information search. *International Journal of Man–Machine Studies, 17,* 87–107.

7

Studying and Annotating Electronic Text

Herre van Oostendorp
Utrecht University
The Netherlands

It is likely that reading texts or hypertexts from computer screens and elaborating these on screen will play an important role in the near future, both in educational settings and in professional settings, such as offices and companies. A complete electronic environment needs to provide users with flexible means to view documents (for instance, to skim or to read more completely), and also with annotation tools and tools to organize and reorganize their annotations, once retrieved (Erickson & Salomon, 1991; van Oostendorp & de Mul, 1992). That also applies to a hypertext environment (Instone, Mynatt Teasley, & Leventhal, 1993). However, there is almost no research on how to annotate electronic information and little empirical data on the effectiveness of electronic annotations. In view of this, the empirical data presented in this chapter are relevant to both educational and professional settings.

The first two studies to be discussed here focus on "student-generated" learning activities (Rickards & August, 1975) in an educational setting; more specifically, the activity examined was note taking during studying. Before introducing these experiments, a few remarks on the role of note taking in learning are in order. Acquiring knowledge from text demands cognitive activity from the reader. The process of acquiring knowledge can be conceived as a continuous sequence of transformations applied to a basic semantic representation (Frijda, 1977). In this approach, the basic semantic representation consists of a more or less connected (hierarchical) network of propositions. These propositions are assigned (interpreted) by the reader after a first reading (van Dijk & Kintsch, 1983). The resulting structure can be made more cohesive in different ways. For instance, by inferring propositions that tie together loosely connected parts, or by constructing an organizing macrostructure. The result is a more cohesive network of information in the memory of the reader. Also, by relating this structure to existing knowledge structures in memory, a richer and more elaborate semantic representation evolves. This can be achieved by activating background knowledge, thinking of examples, anticipating later use of the information, or constructing situation models (mental models) relevant to the information in the text (Ehrlich & Tardieu, 1993; van Oostendorp & Zwaan, 1994). However, this knowledge acquisition process does not always progress smoothly. Sometimes it is possible to facilitate learning by text or teacher interventions (e.g., by clarifying the structure of a text through clarifications in the text itself or by the teacher; Meyer, 1987), and sometimes it is possible to enhance learning by reader or learner interventions, such as the generation of questions, cognitive mapping, underlining, and also note taking.

Note taking is an activity that can play an important role in the knowledge acquisition process, in particular if learners are capable of making adequate notes. In a number of review studies, positive effects of note taking while studying written prose have been reported (Kiewra, 1989; Ladas, 1980). Note taking can increase semantic encoding of presented information, enhance organization in memory, and produce more elaborative learning activities. These kinds of activities contribute to the construction of a more cohesive and more elaborate representation. Apart from this "process" function, a "review" function of notes can be distinguished. Notes may provide subjects with efficient retrieval cues when the subject matter is reviewed. Having notes seems to be very important for an effective reproduction or recall of information (Kiewra, 1989; Rickards & Friedman, 1978). As for the notes, it is not easy to define precisely when notes are adequate. However, several studies have found that the degree of compactness of notes—selecting important information units and writing them down in a few words—is positively related to test performance, especially when the test consists of reproduction or far transfer tasks (Peper & Mayer, 1978, 1986; van Oostendorp & Kok, 1984). In this respect, it seems wise to analyze the notes by the dimension compactness.

TAKING NOTES WHILE STUDYING TEXTS ON A PERSONAL COMPUTER (PC)

The first two studies focused on subjects studying texts which were presented on screen, and typing their annotations on the PC. Although implementation of a note-taking facility on a PC is quite feasible, empirical data regarding the effectiveness of such a system is almost lacking. There are potentially two reasons why note taking could be in general less efficient on a computer. First, there is the problem of typing. In general, when compared to writing, this takes extra time for nonexpert users, because they are likely to be more familiar with the written method of annotation than with any other. A study by Tucker and Jones (1993) showed, for instance, that typing the electronic annotations took more time than writing, and also that fewer annotations were made in the electronic condition. Second, conventional screens have space constraints, that is, displaying the text on screen leaves little space for the annotations. With regard to the technical realization of a note-taking facility, it is difficult to state in advance which form of note taking on screen will give the best results, for instance, in terms of learning. Thus, these studies examined the best technical realization, an important first step.

Different windowing systems were examined. The first study examined simultaneous windows (under or to the left of a text window), and the second study examined alternating windows (subjects could switch back and forth between a text window and notes window which almost totally covered each other). Regarding simultaneous windows, an advantage of a "left" window is that notes can be made next to relevant information in the text, reducing time consuming eye movements and eye regressions (see Fig. 7.1a).

A disadvantage, however, is that only limited space (width) per line is available. An "under" window has the advantage of more space in a line, but the disadvantage of a greater distance between relevant text parts and notes (Fig. 7.1b). It should, however, be tested empirically which interface design gives the best results. On practical (financial) grounds, we omitted a fourth condition, a condition with a right hand window. This omission was based on findings from previous studies (van Oostendorp & Kok, 1984) that subjects preferred note taking in the left margins of books.

An overall advantage of simultaneous note-taking windows is the simultaneous visibility of notes and relevant text parts. Another option is an alternating window (see Fig. 7.2).

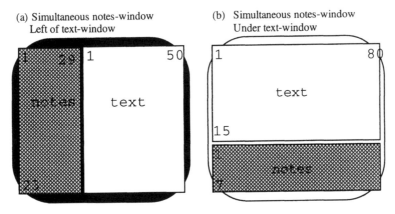

FIG. 7.1. Different window layouts for text and notes (the numbers show the window sizes).

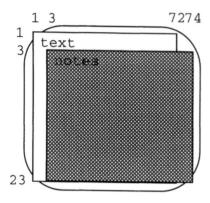

FIG. 7.2.   Alternating window layout
(the numbers show the window sizes).

An advantage of alternating windows is that there are fewer space constraints, and a disadvantage is possibly a higher load on working memory.

The first experiment compared a left and an under computer condition (Fig. 7.1) to a paper and pencil condition. The second experiment compared an alternating computer condition (Fig. 7.2) to a paper and pencil condition.

In both experiments, subjects were undergraduates from the Faculties of Social Sciences and Social Geography at Utrecht University. They had no special screen experience or typing experience, that is, they had no or hardly any computer experience. In Experiment 1, there were 39 subjects with 13 subjects randomly assigned to each condition, and in Experiment 2, there were 36 subjects with 18 subjects randomly assigned to each condition. They participated in the experiments for pay. They were tested individually and were given 30 minutes to study each text.

In the screen conditions, regular personal computers and monitors were used. In Experiment 1, Olivetti M240 personal computers with monochrome 12-inch monitors (resolution 640 × 400 pixels) and in Experiment 2, color 14-inch monitors (resolution 640 × 350) were used. By means of a function key, a subject could switch back and forth between the text windows and notes windows. The text windows and note windows could be scrolled window by window and line by line. Subjects could not make any changes in the text itself. Subjects in the experimental (computer) conditions studied the texts on screen and also took notes on screen by typing them. A control condition studied the texts on paper and also took notes on paper.

The texts were informative texts, approximately 2,000 words. One text was about different forms of justice as described by Max Weber, the other was about conditions for the origin and development of fascism. These texts were selected on the basis of potential interest to the subjects. In the first session, subjects in Experiment 1 had to study both texts, one after the other; in Experiment 2, only one text was presented. In a second session, one week later, subjects took a recall test and a multiple choice test (24 questions) for each text. The test items of the multiple choice test had a high reliability (coefficient alpha varied from .74 to .88). Half of these questions were comprehension questions, the other half factual. Experiment 1 used a cued recall test (12 short answer questions) and Experiment 2 used a free recall test. The free recall score was based on a weighted score, which was the number of idea units recalled multiplied by their weight; the units were weighted from 1 to 4 based on their importance. Expert judges (the author and an assistant) judged the units (334 in total) in terms of importance, and independently, they judged the recall protocols of subjects. The agreement was high ($r = .81$).

The subjects were informed about the purpose of the experiment and the content of the sessions, and that they would be tested one week later in a second session. Subjects were free to take notes or not. Further, they were instructed to take notes in the way they normally would with such a text. The study time of the first session in both experiments was fixed.

Table 7.1 presents the means of the multiple choice test and recall test for both experiments.

An analysis of variance, with condition as the between-subjects factor in both experiments, and text as the within-subjects factor in Experiment 2, showed no significant effects for condition in either experiment. Therefore, the results of these two experiments indicated that learning from screen and taking notes on screen, either in simultaneous or in alternating windows, produces the same or similar learning results as in a traditional paper and pencil method. The general conclusion is that the effectiveness regarding learning performance, of studying texts and typing notes in a computer-supported environment is or can be equal to the effectiveness of a traditional paper and pencil method.

An analysis of the notes showed that subjects in the paper and pencil condition made more notes, and also more compact notes than the subjects in the computer

TABLE 7.1
Mean Percentage Correct for the Multiple Choice Test
and Recall Test for Both Experiments

	Multiple Choice Test	Recall Test
	Experiment 1	
Text 1		
Left simultaneous	51.9	74.7
Under simultaneous	49.4	68.3
Paper & pencil	56.4	66.7
Text 2		
Left simultaneous	41.0	56.8
Under simultaneous	44.2	53.0
Paper & pencil	42.9	59.2
	Experiment 2	
Alternating	59.0	132.7
Paper & pencil	66.0	136.3

conditions ($p < .05$). It was found, for instance, in Experiment 2 that the paper and pencil condition noted more characters than the computer condition, $t(34) = 3.65$, $p < .05$, and also that the compactness was significantly higher, $t(34) = 2.30$, $p < .05$. The compactness score was based on the number of information units multiplied by their importance weight, as in the method of scoring of the free recall protocols, divided by the number of characters used in the notes. I mentioned earlier that this measure has been found to correlate highly with learning performance, such as the free recall scores. It is important to note that the subjects had only little or moderate practice with PCs and with typing. More PC practice and in particular more typing practice could well increase not only the quantity but also the quality of notes. With more experience, subjects can spend more attention and allocate more cognitive capacity to selecting important information units (propositions) and to writing them down in a few words (by applying macrorules such as generalizing, and so on; van Dijk & Kintsch, 1983).

Further, it appeared that the left condition produced more compact notes than the under condition, $t(24) = 2.15$, $p < .05$. In relation to the difference between left as opposed to under, a questionnaire regarding ergonomic user convenience revealed that subjects preferred a left window for making notes, $t(24) = 3.24$, $p < .05$. This questionnaire consisted of several 5-point rating scales such as, "I am content with the way I could make notes" or "I was distracted by the typing of notes." So, a left window may be preferable to an under window when subjects take notes in a window simultaneously with the text. No data are yet available that enable us to directly compare (left) simultaneous and alternating note-taking windows.

Although the learning results in the computer conditions and paper and pencil condition were identical, subjects in the screen conditions indicated that they needed somewhat more time to type their notes than to write them down. In agreement with this, it appeared from an analysis of the notes that the subjects in the computer conditions made less progress in the text than the subjects in the paper and pencil condition.

Annotating Electronic Text With an Electronic Pencil

The third study examined the effects of reading and annotating electronic text with an electronic pencil. Two important advantages of using electronic pencils compared with typing notes can be distinguished. First, a natural and clear distinction between the author's text and a user's notes can be maintained. This is especially relevant to the so-called review phase of note taking (Kiewra, 1989; Rickards & Friedman, 1978); that is, when the text is reviewed, notes may provide users with very efficient retrieval cues, at least when the notes are distinctive from the text. A second, more important advantage regards the annotation technique itself. The typing of notes interrupts processing in an inconvenient way and takes extra time of users compared with writing (Tucker & Jones, 1993). This problem may be overcome by employing a highly overlearned skill like handwriting with an electronic pencil (Wright, 1987, 1988). The third study examined this.

In the present study, a task was used which was representative of a professional setting, for instance, a publishing company. In order to create a realistic task for such a setting, a cognitively demanding variant of a usual proof-reading task (Creed, Dennis, & Newstead, 1988; Wright & Lickorish, 1983, 1984) was designed. In this task, 36 undergraduates had to integrate information from three different texts. They were asked to put themselves in the role of an editor and to judge the presented documents as texts to be edited, and to annotate errors which were included in the texts by the experimenter.

Several types of errors were included: typographic errors—typing errors, omissions, repetitions of a word; syntactical errors—incorrect verb forms; conceptual errors—errors at a local conceptual level; and inconsistencies—conceptual errors between information units on different pages. These errors were included in order to examine the level at which processing difficulties and possible differences between the computer and paper and pencil method occur. It is, for instance, interesting to see whether the conditions differ with regard to performance at a perceptual level (primarily reflected by differences in detecting typographic and syntactical errors), or rather at a cognitive level (primarily reflected by differences in detecting conceptual errors and inconsistencies).

The texts that were used were informative, encyclopedic texts (three pages long, 325 words per page), one about the African elephant, the other about the woodpecker. A few examples of the errors included: typographic—"two kints of elephants . . ." (instead of kinds); syntactical—"some time ago two kinds live . . ." (instead of lived); conceptual—"Elephants are water animals" (instead of land animals); inconsistency—"Elephants are very hairy on their belly" on one page versus "Elephants have very little hair" on another page. The accuracy of annotating the texts for each type of error included by the experimenter was examined by comparing the performance of subjects in the computer condition with the electronic pencil to that of a classical paper and pencil condition. A detected error was only scored as correct if the subjects also had written an adequate correction. It is worthwhile to remark that this punishes those who can spot an error but have no idea of what the right correction might be.

Both software and hardware used was Freestyle developed by WANG. Freestyle is primarily intended to enable the annotation of documents in a way that is similar, by means of the desktop metaphor, to annotations with the use of paper and pencil. By writing with an electronic pencil on an electromagnetic graphic tablet, handwritten annotations can be added to information displayed on screen. A monochrome high-resolution monitor (16-inch) displayed the text with black letters on a white background in A4-format. The monitor was connected to a PC-AT. The texts on screen were scanned in from paper and were, thus, identical in format to the paper version. The annotation technique was explained to the subjects in a preceeding instruction and practice period which lasted approximately 30 minutes. In the actual experiment, each subject was given 15 minutes per text. The experimental variable (computer condition and paper and pencil condition) was introduced in the experiment by means of a within-subjects (latin square) design.

The means for the annotated and corrected errors during processing are presented in Table 7.2.

An ANOVA found no significant effects for condition with regard to annotation of typographic errors, syntactical errors, conceptual errors, or inconsistencies. This indicated that the accuracy of annotating, defined as detection and correction of errors, in the computer condition was equivalent to the annotation accuracy in a traditional paper and pencil condition. This suggests that the perceptual and cognitive aspects of the task were equally difficult for readers when the texts were presented on screen and annotations were made with the electronic pencil as when the texts were presented on paper. A further inspection of the written annotations revealed no differences in number or appearance between the two conditions.

This study focused on only one aspect of annotating electronic documents in a professional setting, namely annotations added for the benefit of the user. In further research, it is worthwhile to concentrate on the communicative aspects of the Freestyle system. Consider, for example, the activities of a secretary who has to process and to correct an already annotated document in an electronic environment. In this case, the annotations have been made by somebody else, and the secretary has to correct the document on the basis of these annotations. I expect that in a situation like this, the paper version of the document including the written annotations can be omitted without reduction of efficiency, accuracy, or satisfaction. The annotations are easy to make and also easy to read. However, empirical data have to provide the evidence.

CONCLUSION

Generally, the three experiments reported here failed to show any differences between conditions in learning performance. This null effect could be attributed to lack of power of the experiments. This is, however, not very plausible for

TABLE 7.2
Mean Number of Annotated and Corrected Errors

Type of Error	Computer	Paper & Pencil
Typographic (0 to 9)	7.2	7.6
Syntactical (0 to 9)	6.5	6.9
Conceptual (0 to 6)	4.9	5.1
Inconsistencies (0 to 12)	7.0	7.7

several reasons. One reason is, for instance, that the test items of the multiple choice and (cued) recall tests were successfully used in other experiments, and showed a high reliability. In view of the reliability problem, in Experiment 1 two texts were used, and in both cases the same conclusion was drawn. Furthermore, the number of subjects used in the experiments was relatively high, certainly in Experiments 2 and 3, compared to other, similar experiments (e.g., Creed et al., 1988; Tucker & Jones, 1993; Wright & Lickorish, 1983, 1984). Experiment 3 used a within-subjects design to control for variability of subjects. Therefore, the present experiments did not lack sufficient power to detect potential effects. In any case, if there are real differences between the computer condition and paper and pencil condition, they are very small.

In view of expected developments in the use of electronic media, these findings are important. Taking notes while reading and studying texts on a PC does not seem to affect performance substantially, even with rather unexperienced subjects and simple screens, and the possibilities of working with an electronic pencil are promising, certainly when users become more experienced with this equipment.

The contribution of this chapter to the main topic of this book *Hypertext and Cognition* is twofold. First, as mentioned earlier, it is important to have note-taking facilities in hypertext systems in order to have a complete electronic environment (see also Erickson & Salomon, 1991; Wilson, 1991). A study by Smeaton (1991) showed, for instance, that the most frequent remarks and suggestions by students for improvement of an information system, including a hypertext, concern facilities to take notes. Of course, the studies reported here isolated only one aspect of the complex situation of information processing. For instance, users also often have to integrate several sources of information (documents, texts, etc.). To support these practices, systems also need facilities for presenting multiple sources of information on screen (van Oostendorp & de Mul, 1992).

Secondly, detailed studies on the best window technique, as done in the first two studies, can provide guidelines for the interface design of hypertext systems. For instance, a left window for notes is probably better than an under window (see the first study). Furthermore, though the studies presented here did not directly compare simultaneous windows to alternating windows, a recent study by Instone et al. (1993) with a hypertext system indicated that simultaneous windows, as opposed to alternating windows, are easier to use, and are leading to better learning results.

In the studies presented here, attention was focused on establishing the equivalence of a computer environment and a paper environment. In future research, it will be interesting to explore potentials that are specific to a computer environment as compared with a paper environment. An example could be enabling hypertext forms of taking notes, even in a hypertext environment (Lachman, 1989).

In the first two studies, the presentation style of the notes windows and text windows was determined by the researcher to enable the examination of effects of either style. In practice, it could be feasible to allow users to choose the style themselves and to customize the way windows are presented, as is the case in most modern operating systems with a graphical user interface, for instance the Apple Macintosh, OS/2, and MS-Windows. However, choosing the right configuration is an extra burden on the workload of users and requires an adequate understanding of the task; users themselves may have trouble with this metacognitive knowledge.

REFERENCES

Creed, A., Dennis, I., & Newstead, S. (1988). Effects of display format on proof-reading with VDU's. *Behaviour and Information Technology, 7*, 467–478.

Ehrlich, M. F., & Tardieu, H. (1993). Modèles mentaux, modèles de situation et compréhension de textes [Mental models, situation models and text comprehension]. In M. F. Ehrlich, H. Tardieu, & M. Cavazza (Eds.), *Les modèles mentaux. Approche cognitive des représentations* (pp. 47–79). Paris: Masson.

Erickson, T., & Salomon, G. (1991). Designing a desktop information system: Observations and issues. *CHI'91 conference proceedings* (pp. 49–54). New York: Addison-Wesley.

Frijda, N. (1977). Kennisverwerving [Knowledge acquisition]. In G. J. Mellenbergh (Ed.), *Rede als Richtsnoer* (pp. 83–98). Den Haag, The Netherlands: Mouton.

Instone, K., Mynatt Teasley, B., & Leventhal, L. M. (1993). Empirically-based re-design of a hypertext encyclopedia. *INTERCHI'93 conference proceedings* (pp. 500–506). New York: Addison-Wesley.

Kiewra, K. A. (1989). A review of note-taking: The encoding-storage paradigm and beyond. *Educational Psychology Review, 1*, 147–172.

Lachman, R. (1989). Comprehension aids for on-line reading of expository text. *Human Factors, 31*, 1–15.

Ladas, H. (1980). Summarizing research: A case study. *Review of Educational Research, 50*, 597–624.

Meyer, B. J. F. (1987). Following the author's top-level organization: An important skill for reading comprehension. In R. J. Tierney, P. L. Anders, & J. N. Mitchell (Eds.), *Understanding reader's understanding: Theory and practice* (pp. 59–77). Hillsdale, NJ: Lawrence Erlbaum Associates.

Peper, R. J., & Mayer, R. E. (1978). Note-taking as generative activity. *Journal of Educational Psychology, 70*, 514–522.

Peper, R. J., & Mayer, R. E. (1986). Generative effects of note-taking during science lectures. *Journal of Educational Psychology, 78*, 34–38.

Rickards, J. P., & August, G. J. (1975). Generative underlining strategies in prose recall. *Journal of Educational Psychology, 67*, 860–865.

Rickards, J. P., & Friedman, F. (1978). The encoding versus the external storage hypothesis in note taking. *Contemporary Educational Psychology, 3*, 136–143.

Smeaton, A. (1991). Using hypertext for computer-based learning. *Computers in Education, 17*, 173–179.

Tucker, P., & Jones, D. M. (1993). Document annotation: To write, type or speak? *International Journal of Man-Machine Studies, 39*, 885–900.

van Dijk, T. A., & Kintsch, W. (1983). *Strategies of discourse comprehension*. New York: Academic Press.

van Oostendorp, H., & de Mul, S. (1992). Integrating information presented in multiple windows. In N. J. I. Mars (Ed.), *Informatiewetenschap 1992* [Information science 1992] (pp. 181–188). Enschede, the Netherlands: STINFON.

van Oostendorp, H., & Kok, I. (1984). Effecten van aanwijzingen voor aantekeningen maken bij HAVO leerlingen [Effects of instruction to take notes with high-school pupils]. *Tijdschrift voor Onderwijsresearch, 9*, 121–135.

van Oostendorp, H., & Zwaan, R. A. (1994). *Naturalistic text comprehension.* Norwood, NJ: Ablex.

Wilson, A. (1991). An overview of the Pen & Pad project. *Golem, Newsletter of Technology and Education, 3,* 10–13.

Wright, P. (1987). Reading and writing for electronic journals. In B. Britton & S. N. Glynn (Eds.), *Executive control processes in reading* (pp. 23–55). Hillsdale, NJ: Lawrence Erlbaum Associates.

Wright, P. (1988). The need for theories of NOT reading: Some psychological aspects of the human-computer interface. In B. A. G. Elsendoorn & H. Bouma (Eds.), *Working models of human perception* (pp. 319–340). London: Academic Press.

Wright, P., & Lickorish, A. (1983). Proofreading texts on screen and on paper. *Behaviour and Information Technology, 2,* 227–235.

Wright, P., & Lickorish, A. (1984). Ease of annotation in proofreading tasks. *Behaviour and Information Technology, 3,* 185–194.

8

▼▼▼▼▼▼▼

Notes on Hypertext, Cognition, and Language

Eric Espéret
University of Poitiers

The purpose of this volume, according to the editors' *Preface*, is to provide a functional, user-centered approach to the issues of hypertext design and usage. As a matter of fact, most chapters in this volume illustrate this approach by examining how actual users interact with information systems in the context of various tasks. The main research questions addressed may be summarized as follows: How does the reader—pupil, student, or professional adult—make use of hypertext in order to reach an objective or goal? What cognitive processes is the reader bringing to bear while doing so? Can hypertext support the tasks for which people have so far used regular printed materials such as books, journals, or technical brochures?

The contributions of the volume are not limited, however, to those fundamental concerns. The chapters also raise central issues related to the design of electronic information systems: size and organization of information units, interface design, ergonomics of retrieval tools. In addition, some chapters address the issue of hypertext application to learning and instruction.

The contributions presented in this volume stress the critical importance of users' cognitive processes, skills, and strategies with respect to the design and use of electronic information systems. A thorough examination of the former is a precondition of the latter's usability.

Within this general framework, three central points have been made throughout the chapters. First, the specificity of hypertext as an information medium lies in its capacity to provide access to information in flexible, nonlinear ways; second, a rational cognitive approach is needed in order to understand the potential of hypertext systems with respect to text processing activities; third, hypertext may promote new ways of designing and writing texts and documents.

In the rest of this chapter, I briefly review each of those points. I discuss the contribution of the volume and stress the issues that are left open for further research. The following comments do not depart from this volume's focus on textual information (as opposed to multimedia), and therefore the term hypertext is used to refer to text-based information systems.

WHAT IS NONLINEAR IN HYPERTEXT?

There is a consensus that the specificity of hypertext rests in its capacity to provide access to information in flexible, or so-called "nonlinear" formats. However, the phrase nonlinear has been used in many different ways and its exact definition, scope, and relevance call for some comments.

Most of the time, documents in hypertext format are said to be nonlinear, in that information can be accessed through different paths; no order of reading is constrained through a unique sequential presentation of paragraphs, or pages, conceived of by the author. According to this view, this is a major difference between hypertext and classical books, the latter being supposedly read from the first page to the last one.

In several chapters of this book, authors have rightfully criticized this view as simplistic or even false. As Dillon pointed out, most printed books include several devices (e.g., page numbers, table of contents, index) that facilitate direct access to the relevant information. It is of interest to find out exactly what linear and nonlinear mean and what aspects of text and hypertext they may concern.

I suggest that the popular definition of linearity—like in some studies of the writing process—results from the confusion of three different features in the processing of verbal information: The organization of lower level language units; the way information is stored in a given medium (book, tape, hypertext, etc.); and the way the reader controls the process of accessing a piece of information.

Both text and hypertext involve the linear ordering of lower level language units. In any natural language, words in sentences are organized in a linear order. Moreover, this order happens to be one of the means used to code syntactic, semantic, and pragmatic options initially taken by the author, with more or less degrees of freedom, depending on the language. Whether a sentence is presented on paper or screen, its lexical units will appear in the same order.

Printed text and hypertext are also similar at the paragraph level, where some further linguistic marks are used to code coherence, like cohesion marks. Linearity of words and sentences, and the meaningfulness of their linear organization, are due to a basic constraint of the human information processing system: You cannot hear or read different words at the exact same time.

Then, the basic units (paragraphs or nodes in hypertext) are physically "stored" (on paper, magnetic tape, hard disk, and so) in a specific order, and can be indexed using this order (page number, date on a time counter, memory address). Storage order constrains the process of accessing information units both in printed and electronic texts, although several differences must be pointed out.

In printed text, the reader has a direct access to the physical storage of information. The problem, however, is to know where a particular piece of information is located, and to actually retrieve that piece of information (i.e., physically manipulate volumes and pages). Several devices, like catalogs, tables of contents, indices, and headings, may assist the reader in that task. The design, implementation, and actual use of these devices will depend on the particular genre of text considered. Manuals and encyclopedia are especially designed to facilitate direct access to any unit. Reading these documents is linear only to the extent that the order of words and sentences is constrained, as discussed earlier. Very few people, however, would ever be interested in reading a dictionary in alphabetic order. Other texts, like novels or epics, call for a linear type of reading and may not include sophisticated direct access devices. These examples illustrate a central point: The design of printed text depends essentially on the usage or task the text is supposed to serve.

In hypertext, the actual storage order is not directly available to readers. A computer takes care of retrieving and displaying the information units. Hypertext systems include several devices that allow easy access to the units, some of which are indeed pretty similar to those found in printed texts (indices, menus, etc.). A significant advantage of hypertext, however, is that the reader is relieved from the burden of physically manipulating the stored information. A selection in a menu automatically results in the display of the selected information. Moreover, hypertext systems include retrieval and navigation tools that just do not have any equivalent in printed books. Examples are string search facilities, embedded links, history trees, and so on.

This brief comparison of printed and electronic texts shows that the opposition of linear and nonlinear formats might be fruitfully replaced by a continuum of flexibility in information access. Different media may involve different forms of flexibility as well. Printed books allow direct manipulation of the physical storage by the reader, but they only provide limited means of selecting, retrieving, and manipulating information. Hypertext does not allow any direct manipulation, but it offers powerful tools for information retrieval.

The core issue for this discussion lies nevertheless in the third feature, that is, reader control over the selection of information units. What the reader needs to do with a text varies according to individual and situational parameters (enjoying a story, seeking a specific information, solving problems, etc.). In any case, the reader's purpose is to build up a satisfactory cognitive text representation. To that end, the reader must choose which information to read first, and which other information is to be processed, until the desired objective is attained. This may involve one or several cycles of information evaluation, selection, and processing (see Rouet & Tricot, in press). The basic problem is not to provide the largest collection of retrieval tools as possible, but to find out which of them may effectively prove helpful in a given situation.

The experiments presented in this volume indicate that some tools or devices may be needed in a large number of cases. For instance, studies by Foltz, Dee-Lucas, and Britt, Rouet, and Perfetti have illustrated a need for top-level structure representation in hypertext. Although this aspect is clearly a central one, the specifics of each task must also be considered. As suggested in the second study by Dee-Lucas, the optimal presentation format may actually depend on the specifics of the reader's task. Different tasks may bring specific requirements: Retrieving a single piece of information without reading irrelevant ones; understanding a device's operating manual, solving usual difficulties yielded by technical terms or spatial layout of components; learning new knowledge in an efficient manner, taking into account one's previous knowledge. The interaction of task requirements and presentation formats, and the qualitative adjustments that may be required to ensure compatibility are important research questions for future studies.

TOWARD A GENERAL COGNITIVE MODEL
OF HYPERTEXT USAGE

The chapter by Rouet and Levonen and the one by Dillon have both pointed out the lack of a general theory and the existence of false or unsupported beliefs about the cognitive processes involved in reading hypertext. It may be interesting to relate those two aspects of this new research area. Most of the myths pointed out by Dillon (e.g., information networks are isomorphic to knowledge structures) may be seen as a consequence of the lack of a theoretical model of hypertext cognitive processing. Just like ancient myths substituted for the understanding of natural phenomena, myths about the so-called "information revolution" are put forward to substitute for an understanding of the cognitive processes involved in the use of information technologies.

So how could these cognitive processes be characterized, and to what extent does hypertext call for new forms of processing?

Whatever the readers' goals may be, text processing amounts to constructing a mental representation based on verbal information. Hypertexts share this general mechanism with traditional, so-called linear texts. In both cases, readers have to access different information units from long term memory and the linguistic message. They have to select, merge, and transform some of the units so as to build up a coherent cognitive representation of the conceptual domain (Espéret, 1992). This fundamental analogy makes it likely that similar basic psycholinguistic capacities, socially learned to make use of written information, are brought to bear both in printed text and hypertext.

Nevertheless, hypertext may also call for more specific abilities, as it offers new ways to display and access textual information. Cognitive studies of text processing have shown that comprehension relies in part on the reader's knowledge of typical text structures (Fayol, 1991; Kintsch & Yarbrough, 1982; Meyer, 1985; van Dijk & Kintsch, 1983). Among other features, textual superstructures are characterized by a particular ordering of text units at several levels: Sentences, paragraphs, and even sections of lengthy texts (Dillon, 1991).

A defining feature of hypertext is to allow new ways of presenting textual information. In doing so, however, hypertext may prevent readers from using their knowledge of typical text structures. Instead, readers will have to learn how to take advantage of different presentation formats, for example, hierarchical access or direct links. This amounts to acquiring new text comprehension strategies, which will be combined with the individual's previous skills.

The chapters in this volume illustrate the necessity for hypertext users to adjust their reading strategies to the specificity of hypertext presentation in three ways. First, Foltz demonstrated subjects' need for textual coherence when reading a hierarchical hypertext. Subjects were reluctant to make long distance jumps in the system, and their navigation patterns showed their concern of maintaining coherence in the information flow. Second, the experiments by Dee-Lucas and Britt, Rouet, and Perfetti showed the need for top-level structural information. Third, several chapters (e.g., Rouet & Levonen) have pointed out the evolution of subjects' strategies with practice. This indicates that the adjustment of the subjects' cognitive strategies to the new characteristics of a medium may take some time, even though novice users can take almost immediate advantage of simple computerized tools (e.g., the note-taking facility studied by van Oostendorp).

Although these findings represent a significant step toward a general model of hypertext processing, they leave a number of issues open. For instance, it is still unclear whether hypertext corresponds to a single superstructural discourse model. It is also unclear what level of processing is actually influenced by hypertext format. In short, a comprehensive psycholinguistic model of hypertext usage (and users) is yet to be proposed.

WRITING HYPERTEXT: WHICH COGNITIVE MODEL?

My final point concerns the issue of designing and writing hypertext. Because of the increasing dissemination of hypertext systems, especially in the areas of education and training, this issue should be much more focused on. Many end users will also be involved in the production or edition of hypertext documents, and one may wonder if this will require new skills, know-how, or strategies on their part. Current theories of writing (e.g., Hayes & Flower, 1980) assume that the end product of writing is a linear, coherent piece of text. Part of the supposed cognitive processes involved in writing are tightly related to these textual aspects (e.g., planning a coherent text sequence).

Given the differences in top-level structure and access methods, writing a hypertext may involve quite different processes. The author must define information units, elaborate a web of semantic connections, and provide top-level representations to facilitate user navigation. So far however, the production of hypertexts is based on common sense heuristics. In many research studies of hypertext (including in this volume), verbal material is extracted from classical linear texts, and then segmented into information units, with little attention paid to the specific requirements of the new presentation format.

If hypertext is to bring the reader new possibilities to make use of textual information, then I would suggest that the cognitive constraints on its production be also considered carefully, in light of current cognitive models of writing. Van Oostendorp (in this volume) has provided evidence that the introduction of notetaking facilities, in a simple computerized information system, can be mastered by inexperienced readers with little apparent difficulty. Beyond this interesting finding, however, ample room is left for thorough investigations of the cognitive processes of planning and composition of hypertext.

CONCLUSION

Hypertext and other types of nonlinear information systems are being spread out at an increasing rate. So far, the focus has been on the design of new systems rather than on the specificity of reading and writing them. This volume represents a welcome shift from system-centered to user-centered research on hypertext. The chapters have addressed a number of central issues: what a model of information usage should look like, the effects of top-level representation, studying multiple documents, and notetaking in electronic environments.

I have identified and discussed three main issues that I believe have emerged from the chapters. First, the traditional opposition between linear and nonlinear texts has been challenged and alternative views have been proposed. Second, elements for a general cognitive model of hypertext processing have been proposed. Third, studying the reading of hypertext should not overshadow the issue of how hypertext is designed and written.

Beyond the individual contribution of the chapters, the volume as a whole provides ample evidence that the association of cognitive theories and empirical research methods can yield a better understanding of how people interact with complex information systems, and hence, contribute to the improvement of the design and use of these systems.

ACKNOWLEDGMENTS

I would like to thank the editors for their useful comments on an earlier draft of this chapter.

REFERENCES

Dillon, A. (1991). Readers' models of text structures: The case of academic articles. *International Journal of Man–Machine Studies, 35*, 913–925.

Espéret, E. (1992). Hypertext processing: Can we forget textual psycholinguistics? In A. M. Oliveira (Ed.), *Structure of communication and intelligent helps for hypermedia courseware* (pp. 112–119). New York: Springer-Verlag.

Fayol, M. (1991). Text typologies: A cognitive approach. In G. Denhiere & J. P. Rossi (Eds.), *Text and text processing* (pp. 61–76). Amsterdam: North Holland.

Hayes, J. R., & Flower, L. (1980). Identifying the organization of writing processes. In L. W. Gregg & E. Steinberg (Eds.), *Cognitive processes in writing* (pp. 3–30). Hillsdale, NJ: Lawrence Erlbaum Associates.

Kintsch, W., & Yarbrough, J. C. (1982). Role of rhetorical structure in text comprehension. *Journal of Educational Psychology, 74*, 828–834.

Meyer, B. J. F. (1985). Prose analysis: Purposes, procedures, and problems. In B. K. Britton & J. B. Black (Eds.), *Understanding expository text.* Hillsdale, NJ: Lawrence Erlbaum Associates.

Rouet, J.-F., & Tricot, A. (in press). Task and activity models in hypertext usage. In H. van Oostendorp (Ed.), *Cognitive aspects of electronic text processing.* Norwood, NJ: Ablex.

van Dijk, T. A., & Kintsch, W. (1983). *Strategies of discourse comprehension.* Hillsdale, NJ: Lawrence Erlbaum Associates.

9

▼▼▼▼▼▼▼

Text and Hypertext

Charles A. Perfetti
University of Pittsburgh

Between text and hypertext there is *hyper*. The question I raise is whether there is something more to connect the two than a common root morpheme.

From the point of view of ordinary reading and text understanding research, hypertext combines the intriguing with the irrelevant. Text research has been prosaic and linear, founded on ordinary cognitive processing assumptions: Words are identified, sentences are parsed, propositions are extracted, meaning structures are built, and so forth. Even the more top-down approaches emphasizing scripts, schemata, and the like use the individual text and reader as the object of study. From such a view, hypertext's intrigue comes from its creative or at least flexible view of texts. They are not objects to be read word for word, or line for line, and certainly not page for page. Texts are points in a space that a learner can explore. That's the intriguing part.

The irrelevant part comes from the tendency of some hypertext research to be technical rather than conceptual, and promotional rather than empirical. Whereas garden variety text research tries to determine how readers understand sentences, build situation models, and make inferences, hypertext research, at least to the uninitiated, tries to persuade that hyper is good and linear is not. There is very little that appears to feed back from hypertext research to fundamental issues of reading or text learning. Even the natural turf of hypertext research, which is learning, fails to get connected. Or so it seems at first glance.

At second glance, and especially if the glance includes the contributions to this volume, a different evaluation is possible. Hypertext and text can be related in some interesting ways and one should expect more connections in the future.

To see these possible connections, we need to reframe the question. The basic division is not one of hypertext versus text, but of process versus use. From this reframing, there follows two overlapping research agendas to which both text and hypertext can contribute.

PROCESSING VERSUS USE

Text research, at least within the cognitive science context, has been largely concerned with how texts are processed (i.e., how understanding is achieved through mental processes that act on text structures and reader knowledge). By contrast, hypertext research has been more concerned with how texts can be used (i.e., how readers function in learning environments with flexible access to texts).

The process–use distinction is multidimensional. Text processing implies generalized cognitive processes that operate across text domains and reader purposes; the latter are important in setting boundaries on the general processes but are not usually viewed as fundamental. Text use assumes a more fundamental role for readers' purposes. Use entails purpose. In a hypertext environment, a reader is trying to learn something, find something, or carry out some task for which access to multiple texts is assumed to be useful. Note also that to ask about hypertext processing seems odd. One does not process texts but uses them for some purposes. Additionally, text processing entails a reader, whereas hypertext use entails a learner or a task performer.

The processing–use distinction is helpful in illuminating different research goals and perhaps basic research assumptions. One might, for example, question whether the assumption of generalized text processing is reasonable. Goals and domains are always relevant, one might argue. To the extent that both text and hypertext environments—reader's goals, text domains, other constraints—are important in influencing the processes readers use, then the difference between text and hypertext reduces considerably. One can use a text to learn (or to do some other task) just as one can use bunches of nonlinear texts to learn (or to do some other task).

Thus, text processing and text use are two distinct, although overlapping kinds of problems in text research. Hypertext research falls naturally into the second category. Text research falls easily into both. Accordingly, it is in research on how people use texts that traditional text research and hypertext research can meet common ground. One can ask the obvious question that researchers, including several authors in this volume, ask: Is nonlinear text more useful for a given task than linear text? But other use questions are interesting as well, and some are more theoretically interesting than the linear–nonlinear question. In the case of single garden variety texts, one can ask about how readers use different kinds of information and the order in which they are used (not always linearly, as Dillon points out in this volume). In all such cases, it is not the distinction between text and hypertext that is fundamental, but whether one is interested in basic processing or in use. The next sections exemplify kinds of text use that can be examined in both text and hypertext research.

Learning and Reasoning

An important use of texts is for reasoning and problem solving. How does a learner use a text in the service of some particular goal? This is a question that can be asked of all kinds of texts in a way that turns from text processing to text use. Reasoning has its own tradition as a fundamental problem in cognition, so we are not tempted to dismiss this use of texts as mere application—a common response of a basic researcher to questions of use as opposed to process.

As one example of a study of reasoning with texts, consider Perfetti, Britt, and Georgi's (1995) study of college students' learning and reasoning about a historical problem. Among other things, this study examined several kinds of text-based reasoning observed in students over a relatively long term period of text study. The essence of text-based reasoning is the use of information in texts to respond to issues of event interpretation and source (text). In history, this can amount to reaching a conclusion about a complex set of events that have been subjected to different interpretations. In addition, a reader can reach conclusions about the texts them-selves—their credibility and their bias. Perfetti et al. (1995) found that students' reasoning about such things was incremental, linked to specific learning, and very malleable. Reasoning was dramatically altered in some cases by what was most recently read. Students were highly influenced by what they read, which ought to be good news for assumptions about text-based learning in school. And, students were generally sensitive to source credibility issues, skilled at picking up text biases even while not free from influence by biased texts.

In the present context, the point of this study is not its specific findings, but its illustration of text-based reasoning. This was a focus not on the processes that readers used in getting information from a text, but rather on the uses that learners made of texts in the service of other goals. It is a question that one might ask as well in hypertext situations, as Britt et al. do in this volume. Asking the question of whether hypertext is better than linear text for such goals may turn out to be less interesting than asking the primary question of how learners integrate information across texts and at the same time keep them separate. This becomes an interesting theoretical as well as applied issue.

MULTIPLE TEXTS AND TEXT REPRESENTATIONS

Text research has traditionally been concerned with single texts, and often very short texts. Hypertext assumes a world of multiple texts. But, as with the process–use distinction, the hypertext–text contrast is not the fundamental one. More important theoretically is how readers represent and use multiple texts.

Whether multiple texts are accessed linearly or nonlinearly is only one question to ask about multiple texts.

Text research has come to acknowledge an important distinction between the representations readers construct of the text itself and the situation described by the text (van Dijk & Kintsch, 1983). Text models contain information that is obtainable from the text with routine language processes, routine knowledge, and routine inference abilities. Situation models add more powerful inferences and richer knowledge. A reader may come to understand and remember a situation, while losing access to the text representation that was instrumental in its construction.

Learning from multiple texts, linear or otherwise, raises interesting additional questions about representations. If a reader reads four different texts about the same topic, is there a single situation model linked to four different text models? Presumably, this is a less than straightforward question. Domain experts, for example, may do better at keeping distinct text models than students. And, empirical testing of such an assumption is difficult. However, merely asking the question creates a link between hypertext and text. Far from being only a problem of application without theoretical interest, hypertext—more generally, multiple text—creates some intriguing theoretical challenges for ordinary text research. Perfetti et al. (1995) argued that multiple text representations must be involved in multiple text learning and that successful learners and reasoners will link models of text arguments to models of situations. Britt, Rouet, Georgi, and Perfetti (1994) proposed such a linking model.

CONTROLLED AND "NATURAL" TEXTS

One final feature of text research relevant to the text–hypertext gap is the kinds of texts used. Because text research in the cognitive tradition has focused on process rather than use, texts have typically been controlled. One might say they have been controlled to the point of dull poverty, but such are the legitimate needs of basic research. Use-directed research is a bit freer to use off-the-shelf texts, modifying them for research purposes but not controlling them. Once again, this is not a matter of a text–hypertext contrast, but a use–process contrast. Again, the Perfetti et al. (1995) study provides a case in point. This study used actual history texts, sparingly modified; furthermore, in another step toward normal use environments, subjects read at home or wherever they chose, not in a lab. Only a study of use can do this, because the questions concern what the students are learning and how they are using what they learn, not how they processed a text.

CONCLUSION

The chapters in this volume represent an interesting sample of the uses of hypertext across research settings. They also include some careful appraisals of the effectiveness of hypertext formats on learning, as well as strong arguments against it. In this brief chapter, I have been more concerned with the question of whether there can be some feedback to basic text research questions from at least some of the user-based hypertext research—whether the gap between hypertext research as applied technology and text research as basic cognition can be bridged a bit. Distinguishing between process and use helps. Mainstream text research can also be about how people use texts to do other things. The use of texts, especially the use of multiple texts, in learning, reasoning, and problem solving brings interesting questions back into the world of theoretical cognition while keeping questions of applications highly visible. This appears to be a useful combination.

REFERENCES

Britt, M. A., Rouet, J.-F., Georgi, M. C., & Perfetti, C. A. (1994). Learning from history texts: From causal analysis to argument models. In G. Leinhardt, I. L. Beck, & C. Stainton (Eds.), *Teaching and learning in history* (pp. 47–84). Hillsdale, NJ: Lawrence Erlbaum Associates.

Perfetti, C. A., Britt, M. A., & Georgi, M. (1995). *Text-based learning and reasoning: Studies in history.* Hillsdale, NJ: Lawrence Erlbaum Associates.

van Dijk, T. A., & Kintsch, W. (1983). *Strategies of discourse comprehension.* New York: Academic Press.

Author Index

163

Subject Index

A

Access, *see* Hypertext, access
Advanced learning, *see* Learning
Analogy, 12, 20, 152
Annotate, 31
  electronic text, 142
Annotations, 137
Apple Macintosh, *see* Computer
Argumentation
  argument models, 68, 69
    global, 47–57
  Argument-based hypertext, *see* Hypertext,
    systems
  arguments and counterarguments, 132
  evidence
    documentary, 43
    primary, 49
    primary and secondary, 58
  legal, 131
Association, 27
  model of human mind, 32
  semantic, 3
Associative
  linking, 28
  paths, 109–110
Attention, 77, 94

B

Background knowledge, *see* Knowledge

Basic semantic representation, *see*
    Representations
Biological hardware, 25
Brown, Professor, 58
Browser, *see* Hypertext, access
Browsing, *see* Navigation
Bush, Vannever, 3
Button, *see* Hypertext

C

CAL terminals, 39
CE+ model, 127
Chapel Hill, 4
Clickable frame, *see* Hypertext, button
Cognitive
  abilities, 5, 114
  constraints, 154
  cost, 14, 17
  differences, *see* Individual differences
  ergonomics, *see* Ergonomics
  implications, 6
  load, 47, 119
  model, 153–154
  processes, 5, 149, 152, 157, 158, 161
  representations, 12, 19, 79, 115–116, 120,
    152
  research tradition, 160
  skills, 7
    using hypertext, 7
  strategies, 70

Printed and bound by CPI Group (UK) Ltd, Croydon, CR0 4YY

17/10/2024

01775683-0019